THE LAI

by

Bishop Ronald Wilson

"From Eden To Heaven"

Copyright 2022
1st Edition
Published by Ronald Wilson Ministries, Inc.
Jefferson, Georgia 30549

All Rights Reserved
Printed in the United States of America

Scriptural quotes in this book are from the King James Version of the Bible. All Punctuation, language style, and spelling of Scriptural passages reflect the KJV.

Mount Of Beatitudes

I recently had a meeting with a dear friend from my childhood days. It was a wonderful time as we reflected on the world we grew up in as kids. It is a huge understatement to say that the world is different today than it was then. Whenever my memories carry me back to those thrilling days of yesteryear, there is one thought I consistently have. I am amazed at how the journey of my life has unfolded. I grew up in a Christian home, with my Dad being a Pastor. You pick up a considerable understanding of the Bible from constant exposure to the Word of God. However, I never imagined as a child that one day, I would be able to visit many of the places I grew up reading about in the Bible.

To walk in the steps of Abraham, Isaac, and Jacob from Old Testament days to walking in the steps of Jesus from New Testament days. Visiting the town of Bethlehem, being baptized in the Jordan River, walking the streets of Jerusalem, and standing on top of the Mount of Olives where Jesus ascended into heaven; were places I could only dream about as a child. And yet, in His divine providence, God allowed me to visit these and numerous other sites on several occasions.

This study is the result of my love of the Bible and history. It combines the two with historical information about several places my travels have carried me and the more important spiritual lessons we can learn from what happened at each location. The intricate way that each place, and the events of that place, are so precisely connected throughout the Bible could not have been concocted in the minds of mere mortal men. So, come along and travel with me to *"The Land of the Bible."*

"The Land Of The Bible"
From Eden To Heaven

~ Introduction ~	9
~ The Garden Of Eden ~	11
~ Mount Ararat ~	15
~ Ur Of The Chaldees ~	19
~ The Tower Of Babel ~	23
~ The Land Of Canaan ~	27
~ From Canaan To Egypt ~	31
~ The Land Of Moriah ~	35
~ Beersheba ~	39
~ Sodom And Gomorrah ~	43
~ The Dead Sea ~	47
~ Hebron And Machpelah ~	51
~ Mount Sinai ~	55
~ Jericho ~	59
~ Hazor ~	63
~ Jerusalem ~	67
~ En Gedi ~	71
~ Beit She'an ~	75
~ Dan ~	79
~ Mount Carmel ~	83
~ Babylon ~	87
~ Assyria ~	91
~ Nazareth ~	95
~ Bethlehem ~	99
~ The Jordan River ~	103

~ The Sea Of Galilee ~ 107
~ Capernaum ~ 111
~ The Mount Of Beatitudes ~ 115
~ The Pool Of Siloam ~ 117
~ Samaria ~ 121
~ The Pool Of Bethesda ~ 125
~ Caesarea Philippi ~ 129
~ Bethany ~ 133
~ Mount Zion ~ 137
~ The Garden Of Gethsemane ~ 141
~ Golgotha ~.. 145
~ Hell Valley ~ 149
~ The Mount Of Olives ~... 153
~ Antioch ~ 157
~ Damascus ~ 161
~ Caesarea ~ 165
~ Athens, Greece ~ 169
~ Corinth ~.. 175
~ Rome ~... 179
~ The Isle Of Patmos ~ 183
~ Ephesus ~... 187
~ Petra ~ 191
~ Megiddo ~ 195
~ Qumran ~ 199
~ Israel ~ 203
~ Heaven ~ 207
~ Epilogue ~ 213

~ Introduction ~

Through the years, I have been blessed to make several trips to *"The Land of the Bible."* I fell in love with the people and the places on my first visit in 1970. When you combine my love of the Bible with my love of history, it probably is no surprise that I love studying the places of the Bible. As I approached the end of a previous study, I thought it would be good to delve into some of the places we read about, but perhaps know very little about. I have not been to all of them, like the first one we will look at, the Garden of Eden. But since it was where everything began for humanity, I thought I would start there.

I hope to present these devotions in an informative and exciting way, describing a small portion of the historical information and making the all-important spiritual application. I pray I can describe these places in a manner that will help all of us in our knowledge of the Bible. So, come along as we begin our journey through the *"The Land Of The Bible."*

~ The Garden Of Eden ~

Genesis 2:8, "And the Lord God planted a garden eastward in Eden, and there He put the man whom He had formed."

When people think about the Garden of Eden, they tend to believe that the garden was Eden, when in fact, the garden appears to have been a small part of a much larger area known as Eden.

In Hebrew, Eden means "place of pleasure and delight." During the creation process, we see the ultimate act of creation was man. God lovingly formed him from the dust of the earth and breathed into him the breath of life. It was indeed a place of pleasure and delight because of Adam and Eve's relationship with God and each other. This special place was made for them and their descendants to enjoy. Unfortunately, Adam and Eve would be the only ones to enjoy this garden of delight.

Genesis 2:9 says, "And out of the ground made the Lord God to grow every tree that is pleasant to the sight, and good for food; the tree of life also in the midst of the garden, and the tree of knowledge of good and evil." While we often focus on just two trees, this verse lets us know that God provided every kind of fruit they would need, placing only one restriction upon them. They could not eat the fruit from the Tree of the Knowledge of Good and Evil. They could have eaten the fruit from the Tree of Life, but they chose not to and instead chose the one thing they were forbidden to eat. Their disobedience would plunge the world into sin.

While we may never fully understand why they did this, I think we should at least consider one possibility. The serpent, whom we know as Satan, at some point in the dateless past allowed his heart to be filled with pride and rebellion to the point that he decided to overthrow God and become God himself. He failed, and as a result Revelation 12:9 tells us he was cast down to the earth. Adam and Eve were the prized creation of God. In Satan's temptation of Eve, he convinced her that if she ate this fruit, she would become like God. We could say that Satan was attempting in another form to overthrow God.

It ultimately came down to a choice between obedience and disobedience. If Adam and Eve had eaten the fruit from the Tree of Life, they could have lived forever. If they ate the fruit from the Tree of the Knowledge of Good and Evil, they would die. The choice was between life and death. Unfortunately, in their disobedience they chose death over life.

The question before us today is the location of the Garden of Eden. Genesis 2:10-14 says, "And a river went out of Eden to water the garden; and from thence it was parted and became into four heads. The name of the first is Pison: that is it which compasseth the whole land of Havilah, where there is gold; And the gold of that land is good: there is bdellium and the onyx stone. And the name of the second river is Gihon: the same is it that compasseth the whole land of Ethiopia. And the name of the third river is Hiddekel: (Tigris) that is it which goeth toward the east of Assyria. And the fourth is Euphrates."

According to verse 10, only one river flowed out of Eden into the garden. At some point, after leaving the garden it split into four rivers. Of the four rivers mentioned, we only know where two of them are today, and their headwaters come from southeastern Turkey. Both of them flow south, eventually emptying into the Persian Gulf. It is also in this same area where Mount Ararat is located.

So, how far had people moved from Eden before the flood and how far did the ark float during the flood? Are we looking at a considerable distance or was the land of Eden somewhere near Mount Ararat?

Some say the Garden of Eden is beneath the waters of the Persian Gulf. A map of that region shows a river that empties into the Persian Gulf. The Shatt al-Arab River is about 120 miles long and is formed by the merging of the Tigris and Euphrates Rivers. All three of these rivers flow from north to south. For the Garden of Eden to be buried beneath the waters of the Persian Gulf, the rivers would have to flow south to north which they do not.

Several years ago, I saw a satellite image of that part of the world which showed four rivers coming from the southeastern part of Turkey. They flowed through what we know as the "fertile crescent." Two of those rivers still exist, but two are dry riverbeds. I have tried to find that photo but to this point I have not been successful.

For the rivers to reach the areas described in the Book of Genesis, they must have their origin somewhere north, in the mountainous region of southeastern Turkey, which is exactly what that image showed. Since scholars cannot agree on the location of Havilah, which the Bible says the Pison River flows into, it doesn't matter whether Havilah is on the east or the west side of the Red Sea if the waters are flowing from the north. We should also bear in mind that the massive destruction the flood would have caused could have significantly altered the landscape.

While we can debate the location, let us never forget what happened in the Garden of Eden. In a place where God provided everything they needed, Adam and Eve chose to disobey God by partaking of the one thing He told them not to. As a result, sin entered the world, bringing separation from God, a loss of innocence, pain in childbearing, and the cursing of the ground. They were driven from the beautiful Garden of Eden and the entire world was plunged into sin. They could have chosen life, but instead, they chose death.

I'm thankful that God loved us enough to provide a remedy for our sin when He sent His only begotten Son into the world. Jesus took upon Himself the sins of the world, making it possible for us to have everlasting life. Do you know Jesus as your personal Lord and Savior? If not, today is a great day to repent of your sins and invite Him into your heart. God is preparing an eternal land of Eden for those who become part of the family of God, and I'm looking forward to seeing it one day.

~ Mount Ararat ~

In our previous devotion, I mentioned that some people believe the Garden of Eden was located beneath what is now the waters of the Persian Gulf. I posed the question as to how far the Ark may have floated during the flood. The mountain we know as Mount Ararat is almost one thousand miles from the Persian Gulf. It would not be impossible for a boat to float that far in a little over a year, but did it?

While there is one mountain today designated as Mount Ararat, the Bible actually says, "the mountains of Ararat," which again points to an area that included several mountains, much like Eden was a larger area that contained the garden. Both Eden and Ararat are in the same area of modern-day southeastern Turkey from where the Tigris and Euphrates Rivers flow.

Some believe they found the remains of the Ark on one of these mountains. The mountain where they believe they found it is a 17,000-foot-high volcano. While Noah had no control over where the Ark landed, God did, and I tend to believe that He would have stopped it in a place where it would have been easier for Noah and his family, as well as all the animals, to disembark.

We have no idea how much the landscape may have changed because of the flood, but if they stayed in the same proximity to Eden, the mountains of Ararat would have been a familiar landmark to them.

There is evidence of people who lived in this area about that time. They became known as the Kingdom of Urartu, or the Kingdom of Van. Lake Van still exists today. These people would later find themselves in constant warfare with the Assyrians as both nations were trying to expand their borders. It could have been this continual warfare that caused some of the inhabitants to move southward to the land of Ur.

As I mentioned in the devotion on the Garden of Eden, the location of Mount Ararat is not the most important issue. What's important is that one year and ten days after the windows of heaven were opened and the fountains of the deep were broken up, Noah and his family walked safely out of the Ark.

They survived because Noah believed God. It not only seemed foolish to everyone else when Noah first started building the Ark, it probably seemed foolish to Noah and his family. Sin entered the world through Adam and Eve's disobedience, but Noah's obedience saved humanity from total annihilation. Both choices had massive repercussions. The choices we make each day affect us, our family, and those around us.

When God spoke to Noah and told him to build the Ark, some believe it had never rained at this point in history. They point to Genesis 2:5-6, "And every plant of the field before it was in the earth, and every herb of the field before it grew: for the Lord God had not caused it to rain upon the earth, and there was not a man to till the ground. But there went up a mist from the earth and watered the whole face of the ground." Those verses clearly say it had not rained up until that point in time, but that was before sin entered the world. What were the full consequences of sin? We know the curse of sin affected the world, but to what extent did the curse affect the weather?

We also have to consider that, as far as we know, Noah was building a rather large boat on dry land with no way to move it to the closest body of water. I'm sure Noah was ridiculed, but he persevered through the mockery and finished what God told him to build. He built it according to God's specifications, and it withstood the flood. After the waters had subsided, God let the Ark land safely somewhere in the mountains of Ararat.

The Ark reveals both the judgment and the mercy of God. The world of our day believes we are foolish for obeying God rather than living like them. Many have convinced themselves they can live any way they choose and that they are not accountable to anyone. Some think they can hide their sin. But Genesis 6:5 says, "And God saw that the wickedness of man was great in the earth, and that every imagination of the thoughts of his heart was only evil continually." God sees what we do and one day we will be held accountable for how we have lived.

Jesus said in Matthew 24:37 that the world will be living as they were in the days of Noah when He returns. So many people today live a wicked and perverted lifestyle and don't even want to consider the existence of God. In some parts of the world, people suffer great persecution for being a Christian. But rest assured, one day it will be worth whatever we may have to endure when we land safely on the shores of sweet deliverance.

~ Ur Of The Chaldees ~

At some point, people began making their way south from the land of Eden. Many stopped in the area where the Tower of Babel would later be built. The Tigris and Euphrates rivers flow through this region before merging and forming one river that makes its way to the Persian Gulf. The places we have looked at to this point are in an area known as the fertile crescent. With their abundant water source, these rivers made it possible for people to plant crops and build homes.

Biblically speaking, we know very little about Ur, except it is where a man named Abram lived. It was located in a region known as Mesopotamia. It is sometimes referred to as "the land between the rivers." It was the birthplace of the first major civilizations after the flood and is often referred to as "the cradle of civilization." The oldest known four-wheel wagon was found in Ur. Things we take for granted, such as writing, the wheel, a code of laws, the sail, the concept of the 24-hour day, and the irrigation of crops, were first developed in the land between the rivers. On August 23rd, 1921, the name for most of this area was changed to Iraq.

The Sumerians, Babylonians, Persians, and Assyrians became great nations in this area. The impact they made on the world of their day is difficult to comprehend. In fact, their influence is still being felt today. Unfortunately, in a relatively short period of time after the flood, humanity again turned away from the One True God and began to worship the gods they created with their own hands.

In this land of pagan worship, God spoke to Abram, who we know better as Abraham, and began a relationship with him that would change the world. While I will deal more extensively with that in the following devotion, it's important to understand that Abram grew up surrounded by all these man-made gods, which are said to have numbered over one thousand.

Several historical documents state that Abram's father was a high priest in the Babylonian cult. Numerous historical records show how wicked this belief and form of worship were.

I have often wondered how Abraham came to the knowledge of Yahweh? How was he able to sort through all the religious voices he grew up with and get back to the God who created all things? While this is one of the unanswered questions of the Bible, the issue it presents is one that requires an answer from each of us. We live in a sinful day. Voices denying the One True God are speaking loudly in our generation, while at the same time worshipping gods of their own making. The gods of this generation may not be chiseled out of stone or whittled out of wood, but they are nonetheless gods. Many worship fame, money, sex, the accumulation of material things, and a multiplicity of other things. They are every bit as much a god as the idols people worshiped in the past.

There came a point in the relationship God wanted to build with Abraham that He told him to pack his bags and begin a journey. While the cities of that day certainly do not measure up to the standards of our day, it's worth noting that God was calling him to leave a place of civilization that probably provided a level of prosperity and comfort. Some of the ancient cities were rather well developed. God was calling Abraham to walk away from that and adopt the lifestyle of a Bedouin. The only clear understanding he had of where he would eventually settle is summed up in Hebrews 11:10, "I'm looking for a city, which hath foundations, whose builder and maker is God."

In many respects, our journey is much like Abraham's. We never know where the twisting roads of life may carry us, but our eternal destination is the place God is preparing for all His children. The challenge is to trust and obey the call of God, even when we don't understand. Heaven will be worth whatever sacrifices we have to make in this world.

~ The Tower Of Babel ~

Some people try to attack and discredit everything in the Bible, but every now and then, they run up against something with an abundance of secular history which verifies the Biblical account. The tower of Babel is one of them. Sinful humanities attempt to explain the multitude of languages often leaves more questions than answers. In contrast, the Bible narrative which credits God with the gift of language and the vast diversity of cultures gives a clear and easily understood explanation.

The Tower of Babel is known as a place of rebellion against God. It was built in a foolish attempt to ascend into heaven so that, at the least, they would be equal with God, with the ultimate intent to overthrow God and kill Him if possible. Does that sound familiar? Isaiah 14:12-13, "How art thou fallen from heaven, O Lucifer, son of the morning! how art thou cut down to the ground, which didst weaken the nations! For thou hast said in thine heart, I will ascend into heaven, I will exalt my throne above the stars of God." Satan failed in his attempt to overthrow God; Nimrod and the Babylonians also failed.

Nimrod was Noah's great-grandson. Noah was most likely still alive when Nimrod was born, so the account of the flood and how God saved them while judging a sinful world have been a commonly discussed event. Nimrod should have known better, but humanity's conceit and sinful lifestyle that existed pre-flood resurfaced and increased dramatically under his leadership. The historian Josephus says that Nimrod's building of the tower was an effort to build a structure so tall that it would survive another flood. In a way, it was Nimrod saying that I will build something so tall that even God can't destroy it. Nimrod proclaimed himself to be god and demanded worship, and thus was born the Babylonian cult.

God decided to break their arrogance by destroying their ability to communicate with one another. Jewish historians say God confused the people by splitting them up into seventy different nations and tribes, each with its own language. When they were dispersed all over the world, they carried with them the belief that had been birthed in Babel. When you sort through the translations and customs of the various lands they settled, you are unmistakably taken back to the Tower of Babel, down to the most minute details of how they worshiped. This form of worship still occurs in many parts of the world today.

When the tower was abandoned, they began to focus their attention on building the city of Babylon. Babylon epitomizes sinful living, perverted lifestyles, rebellion against God, the worship of false gods, and anything else that is anti-God and anti-Christ. Babylonian worship rears its ugly head one final time in the last days, both as a city and a religion.

As I mentioned in our previous devotion, it is believed by some that Abram's father was a high priest in the Babylonian cult. The Bible clearly states that Terah worshipped other gods. Joshua 24:2, "And Joshua said unto all the people, Thus saith the Lord God of Israel, Your fathers dwelt on the other side of the flood in old time, even Terah, the father of Abraham, and the father of Nachor: and they served other gods." God wanted Abraham to get out of this wicked and sinful area.

We can learn many lessons from the Tower of Babel, but let me quickly sum them up like this. When God instructed Noah to build an ark, it was God providing a means of salvation from the coming destruction of the flood. When Nimrod began the Tower of Babel, it was his attempt to provide his own salvation. He was basically saying, I don't need God; I can do this my way. The spirit of Babylon is one of rebellion against God.

While we may not build a literal tower today, we often think that by good works, by attending church, and by being a mostly moral person, I can create my own salvation without God's help. But true salvation is found only from God through Jesus, who came to give us life. I urge you to accept Jesus as your Savior while you still have time.

~ The Land Of Canaan ~

At first glance, it appears that Abraham and his family took an indirect route to Canaan until you realize that had they gone directly west from Ur, they would have gone through portions of the Arabian and Syrian Deserts. They would also have to find their way through the formidable mountains that separate Jordan from Canaan. The route they chose kept them in the fertile crescent, which would have been a more pleasant journey.

Based on what we read in Genesis 11:31, Abraham's father Terah initiated the first part of the journey. Genesis 11:31, "And Terah took Abram his son, and Lot the son of Haran, his son's son, and Sarai his daughter in law, his son Abram's wife; and they went forth with them from Ur of the Chaldees, to go into the land of Canaan; and they came unto Haran and dwelt there."

The people of Haran worshipped the same false gods as did the people in Ur of the Chaldees, so stopping in Haran was probably not much different than Ur. Pagan worship was still the norm. As we discussed previously, the Bible says that Terah worshipped and served these gods. (Joshua 24:2)

While Terah may have been involved in the initial move, it's clear from Genesis 15:17 that God's call to Abraham began in Ur. "And He (God) said unto him, (Abraham) I am the Lord that brought thee out of Ur of the Chaldees, to give thee this land to inherit it." Nehemiah 9:7 confirms that. "Thou art the Lord, the God who didst choose Abram, and broughtest him forth out of Ur of the Chaldees, and gavest him the name of Abraham."

The place God intended for Abraham to settle is known as Canaan. Genesis 12:5, "And Abram took Sarai his wife, and Lot his brother's son, and all their substance that they had gathered, and the souls that they had gotten in Haran; and they went forth to go into the land of Canaan; and into the land of Canaan they came."

Exodus 3:17 describes it as a place "flowing with milk and honey." Some say the name is derived from Noah's grandson, Canaan. Though small, Canaan was a strategic piece of land. With the Mediterranean Sea to its west and the Jordan River to its east, it connected some of the great world powers of that day.

Egypt was the breadbasket of the ancient world. When crops were harvested, they were sent north up two major International Trade Routes. One was called the "Via Maris" or "the way of the sea," because it was next to the Mediterranean Sea. The second one is a road that probably all of you have heard about. It was the "Kings Highway." I've had the privilege to travel both of these highways. Egypt was the major supplier for the Hittites, the Assyrians, the Babylonians, the Persians, and other nations that we read about in the Bible.

The ancient world understood that if you wanted to control the world of their day, you had to control these international roads. That is part of the reason why this area has seen so many battles. The land bridge of Canaan was the lifeblood between Asia, Africa, and Europe. Even during the days of the Roman Empire, which played a significant role in the events of the New Testament, this piece of land was crucial. Due to the oil rich deposits in that part of the world, it is still a land upon which the eyes of the world are focused on a daily basis.

For Abraham and his descendants, Canaan was the land of promise. It was God's gift to His people. Genesis 17:7-8, "And I will establish My covenant between Me and thee and thy seed after thee in their generations for an everlasting covenant, to be a God unto thee, and to thy seed after thee. And I will give unto thee, and to thy seed after thee, the land wherein thou art a stranger, all the land of Canaan, for an everlasting possession; and I will be their God." This covenant promise God made with Abraham also plays a huge part in the controversy that continues to rage in that part of the world today.

Canaan represents a place of rest. While there doesn't seem to be much rest in that part of the world today, there is an eternal land of Canaan that God has promised to all who follow Him, and it will far surpass the land where Abraham and his descendants settled. We even sing about it, "I'm Bound For The Land Of Canaan."

Just as the covenant God made with Abraham and his descendants is steadfast, so is His promise to His children who have put their trust in Jesus. Sometimes the journey gets rough, as it did with Abraham, but if we hold fast and endure whatever may come our way, it will be worth it all.

~ From Canaan To Egypt ~

In Genesis chapter 12, Abraham leaves Haran and goes into Canaan to possess the land God promised him. Abraham built altars to worship God at the various places where he would temporarily set up camp. Things seemed to be going well until this happened. Genesis 12:10, "there was a famine in the land: and Abram went down into Egypt."

Although Abraham trusted God enough to begin a journey, not knowing where he was going, he made a decision that appears to have been solely his own when faced with famine. There is no indication from the Bible that God told Abraham to go to Egypt. Instead of trusting God to provide for him where he was, he made a decision, the effects of which have rippled rather loudly down through history. In his fear, Abraham seems to have forgotten the promise and covenant God made with him.

This was not the last time a famine would cause God's people to go to Egypt. This occasion caused Abraham to tell a lie, well, actually a half-lie, if such a thing exists. The Bible says that his wife Sarah was a very attractive lady. Abraham feared that her beauty would cause someone to kill him so they could take his wife. He convinced her to tell everyone that she was not his wife, but his sister. This was a half-truth because Abraham and Sarah had the same father but different mothers. (Genesis 20:12)

God intervened and Abraham's life was spared, but this trek into Egypt set a pattern that just two generations later would cause his family to move to Egypt and it would be nearly four hundred years before they would be able to leave. In a relatively short period of time, they went from the inhabitants of the land of promise to slavery.

But something else happened in Egypt that would have even greater repercussions on world history. Genesis 16:1, "Now Sarai Abram's wife bare him no children: and she had a handmaid, an Egyptian, whose name was Hagar." Abraham seems to have left Egypt with much more than he had when he went there, including a handmaid named Hagar.

When Sarah convinced herself that she would never have any children of her own, in a moment of weakness she devised a plan contrary to God's will; she persuaded Abraham to have a child with Hagar. It was Sarah's idea, but the consequences of her idea, combined with Abraham's willingness to follow through with it, still plague the world. The warfare that began more than three thousand years ago between Abraham's promised seed and the Egyptian handmaid's seed continues until this day. It began with a trip to Egypt.

The decisions we make can have long-lasting effects. Even though Abraham had a son before Isaac, God said the promise would be fulfilled through Sarah's son, not Hagar's son. Genesis 17:19-21, "And God said, Sarah thy wife shall bear thee a son indeed; and thou shalt call his name Isaac: and I will establish My covenant with him for an everlasting covenant, and with his seed after him. And as for Ishmael, I have heard thee: Behold, I have blessed him, and will make him fruitful, and will multiply him exceedingly; twelve princes shall he beget, and I will make him a great nation. But My covenant will I establish with Isaac."

In just three verses, a significant portion of the genealogy of the Middle East is established. It also clearly states the covenant God established with Abraham would pass through the descendants of Isaac, not Ishmael. You can't help but wonder how much of the trouble the world has experienced could have been avoided if Sarah had not suggested that her husband have a child with another woman. And yet, it is what it is.

This story reminds us that our decisions have consequences. Some are not as serious as others, but they all have the potential to alter our lives and the lives of those around us. Abraham had been called out of a sinful world to live a life that was sanctified and dedicated to God. In his fear, in his attempt to preserve his life, rather than trusting God to provide for him, he took a detour that would cause him great grief. Although it may be hard to see where we are when we are in the midst of a famine, God always has a better plan than anything we can devise on our own.

~ The Land Of Moriah ~

Moriah is a beautiful word to me because of what happened here during three major events of the Bible. Moriah is described as a land, just as Eden was. This means that the land of Moriah encompasses an area larger than just one mountain.

We are first introduced to Moriah in one of the most emotional stories in the Bible. Genesis 22:2, "Take now thy son, thine only son Isaac, whom thou lovest, and get thee into the land of Moriah; and offer him there for a burnt offering upon one of the mountains which I will tell thee of." I cannot begin to imagine how Abraham must have felt. The covenant God made with Abraham depended upon him having descendants to pass it on to. Isaac was that covenant son. And yet, in the most incredible act of faith, Abraham set out to do what God asked him to do. Hebrews 11:17-19, "By faith Abraham, when he was tried, offered up Isaac: and he that had received the promises offered up his only begotten son, Of whom it was said, That in Isaac shall thy seed be called: Accounting that God was able to raise him up, even from the dead."

When Isaac saw they had everything they needed for a sacrificial offering except a lamb, he asked his father, "where is the lamb." Abraham responded in Genesis 22:8, "My son, God will provide Himself a lamb." Little did Abraham know how prophetic his statement was, not just for Isaac, but through Jesus, it was for the world.

The second time we are introduced to Moriah is in 2 Chronicles 3:1, "Then Solomon began to build the house of the Lord at Jerusalem in Mount Moriah." There came a day when David saw something he felt needed to be rectified. 1 Chronicles 17:1, "Now it came to pass, as David sat in his house, that David said to Nathan the prophet, Lo, I dwell in an house of cedars, but the ark of the covenant of the Lord remaineth under curtains." God would not allow David to build the temple because He wanted it to be built by a man of peace instead of a man of war. Rather than having a pity party because he couldn't build it, David immediately began assembling everything his son Solomon would need to fulfill that dream. We may have a dream that we never realize personally, but we can do everything possible to make sure that someone else sees that dream become a reality. And so, about one thousand years after Abraham and Isaac climbed Mount Moriah, Solomon built a temple on that exact spot. It was so magnificent that the world still talks about it today.

That brings us to the third and most eternally significant event, the crucifixion of Jesus. Mount Moriah was where Abraham took Isaac to offer him as a sacrifice, and Mount Moriah was where Solomon built the temple. Although Solomon's Temple was destroyed, a second temple was built on the original site. During the earthly ministry of Jesus, Herod had refurbished the second temple and it was once again a magnificent place of worship.

So, where was Jesus crucified? At the beginning of this devotion I mentioned that Moriah was more than just a single mountain. There are two traditional places where Jesus could have been crucified, both of which are in the "land of Moriah." The moment Jesus died on Golgotha, the veil in the temple on Mount Moriah was torn asunder. In the past, only a limited number of people had access into the Holy of Holies. The sacrifice of Jesus made it possible for every born-again believer to approach the throne of God boldly.

In 70 A.D., the Romans destroyed the second temple on Mount Moriah. The only thing that remains is the Western Wall, often called the Wailing Wall. The Dome of the Rock sits on top of Mount Moriah today. I was able to go inside the Dome of the Rock on one of my visits, but it is now closed to non-Muslims.

The Bible speaks of a third temple that will be built on the same spot where Abraham went to offer Isaac, where Solomon built his temple, and where the veil was rent when Jesus died for our sins. With every passing day, we are getting closer to the time when the events of the last days will unfold and Jesus will return. Are you ready for that day? If not, please accept Jesus as your Savior. He's waiting for you to ask.

~ Beersheba ~

Several places seemed to have been favorite locations for Abraham to set up camp; Beersheba was one of them. I have been blessed on several occasions to visit the ruins of this ancient city. It is an amazing experience to know that you are walking on the same cobblestone streets that Abraham, Isaac, and Jacob walked.

Abraham's household was of considerable size. According to Genesis 14:14, Abraham had 318 trained servants who were born in his household. This number does not reflect their wives and children. They fought to free Abraham's nephew Lot when he was captured, pursuing Lot's captors to the city of Dan, one of the northernmost cities in Canaan. Beersheba was one of the southernmost cities, so you often hear the expression, "from Dan to Beersheba." The distance from between these two cities was approximately 150 miles.

Beersheba is mentioned in Genesis chapter 21 in connection to several significant events. In verse 14, we see that Sarah no longer wanted Hagar and Ishmael around due to the jealousy that had erupted between her and Hagar. Reluctantly, Abraham sent Hagar away. She and her son wandered in the desert around Beersheba. Trouble was already brewing between Isaac, Ishmael, and their descendants.

In Genesis chapter 20, Abraham encountered Abimelech, the King of Gerar, while traveling through the southern region of Canaan. Once again, fearing for his life, Abraham told the same lie he told in Egypt. When Abimelech saw that Abraham's wife was beautiful, he took her into his harem, not knowing that she was married to Abraham. Because of this, God put a curse on Abimelech's household and warned him in a dream that Sarah was married. Abimelech quickly returned Sarah to her husband along with a generous peace offering. To defend himself, Abraham clearly stated in Genesis 20:12, "And yet indeed she is my sister; she is the daughter of my father, but not the daughter of my mother; and she became my wife."

In Genesis 21:25, Abraham and Abimelech meet again; this time the conflict is over a well. Some of Abimelech's servants had "violently" taken away the well in Beersheba that belonged to Abraham. Abimelech was unaware that this had happened, so a treaty was established that Abraham secured by giving Abimelech seven lambs. It became known as "the well of the treaty" and later as "the well of the seven."

Beersheba also figures in the story of Abraham's son, Isaac. There was another famine in Canaan. This time God plainly told Isaac to stay out of Egypt. Genesis 26:2, "And the Lord appeared unto him, and said, Go not down into Egypt; dwell in the land which I shall tell thee of." Just as Abraham told Abimelech that Sarah was his wife, Isaac now does the same with Rebekah. But their conflict does not end there.

Isaac discovered that the wells his father's servants dug had been filled with dirt by the Philistines. He reopened those wells and dug new ones. (Genesis 26:18-22) After that, Isaac went to Beersheba. The Lord appeared to him as He had with his father Abraham and made him the same promise of many descendants. In a repeat performance, Abimelech arrived and asked for another treaty with Isaac, identical to the one made with

Abraham. Isaac agreed. Beersheba became the name of the town near the wells that Abraham and Isaac dug.

Isaac (Genesis 26:24) and Jacob (Genesis 46:2) both heard from God in dreams they had at Beersheba.

Beersheba was the place where Samuel's two wicked sons served as leaders. (1 Samuel 8:1-3) This perversion of their judgeship led Israel to demand a king. (1 Samuel 8:6–9) By the time of the reign of King Uzziah, Beersheba seems to have become a center of false worship. The Prophet Amos warned those who wanted to truly worship the Lord, "Do not journey to Beersheba." (Amos 5:5)

Today, the spot where Beersheba once stood is marked by ancient ruins.

~ Sodom And Gomorrah ~

The very mention of Sodom and Gomorrah immediately brings to mind the judgment and sudden destruction that was the result of perversion and sin of the highest order. It is a sin that attacks the most basic plan of God from the dawn of creation in that a man and a woman should marry and have children. That is God's natural order of relationships. It is unnatural and unfruitful when two of the same gender try to form a marriage relationship. One can consider themselves the husband and the other the wife, but they will never produce offspring.

Let me hasten to add that God "is not willing that any should perish, but that all should come to repentance." (2 Peter 3:9) God will judge the wicked, but He extends mercy to the righteous.

Sodom is first mentioned in Genesis chapter 10 where a brief genealogy of Noah's family is mentioned. No additional information is given; we just know that Sodom already existed during this time.

In Genesis chapter 13, when Lot was given the option to take the land of his choosing, he saw the plains of Jordan were well watered, and the Bible adds, "even as the garden of the Lord." Is this verse saying that the place around Sodom was so fertile that it was compared to the Garden of Eden? Regardless of how fertile and lush the landscape may have appeared; the very next verse tells us the men of Sodom were exceedingly wicked sinners. That's what Lot should have seen. Why would Lot even consider living in a place of such sin?

From Genesis chapter 14, we know that Sodom was in the vicinity of the Dead Sea. It is referred to in verse 3 as the "salt sea." In a strange twist of fate, Abraham befriended the people of Sodom and Gomorrah. As the result of a battle, Abraham's nephew Lot was captured. When Abraham fought for his release, it was so beneficial for the inhabitants of Sodom and Gomorrah that they wanted to reward Abraham for what he had done, but he refused to take what they offered. Genesis 14:23, "I will not take from a thread even to a shoelatchet, and that I will not take any thing that is thine, lest thou shouldest say, I have made Abram rich."

The story that most are familiar with is found in Genesis chapter 18, where God again confirms that the sin of Sodom and Gomorrah was very grievous. At this point, Lot had moved into the city and became a respected leader. Genesis 19:1 says, "Lot sat at the gate of the city." This is where leaders assembled, offered advice, passed laws, and gave judgment. In Genesis chapter 23, Abraham negotiated the purchase of the Cave of Machpelah as a tomb for his wife Sarah, at the city gates of Hebron. In Ruth chapter 4, Boaz exercised his right as a kinsman-redeemer at the gate of Bethlehem. Lot was a man of influence in Sodom. Sadly, his influence had no impact on them changing their sinful lifestyle.

Abraham pleads with God for mercy. While Abraham's reaction may have been affected in part due to Lot living there, I believe a greater Biblical truth is being expressed. In Genesis 18:25, Abraham made a statement that can be viewed as a question, but it can also be viewed as a statement of his faith in God. "shall not the Judge of all the earth do right?"

Archeologists believe they have discovered where Sodom and Gomorrah were located, near the southern part of the Dead Sea. It is distinguished by an area filled with brimstone. If you strike a match to the rocks in that area, they will begin to burn. The unmistakable smell of sulfur will sting your nose. Deuteronomy 29:23, "And that the whole land thereof is brimstone, and salt, and burning, that it is not sown, nor beareth, nor any grass groweth therein, like the overthrow of Sodom, and Gomorrah."

2 Peter 2:6 tells us the judgment of Sodom and Gomorrah is an example of what will happen to all who sin and live ungodly lives. Jude verse 7 tells us the way Sodom and Gomorrah were judged is an example of the eternal judgment that sinners will face.

God wants to extend mercy, but we must repent and turn from sin.

~ The Dead Sea ~

I mentioned the Dead Sea briefly in my previous devotion. This area is unique for several reasons. It is the lowest place on earth, more than 1,300 feet below sea level. It also is the saltiest sea on earth, having more than ten times the salt content of the oceans. The ocean has about 3% salt content; the Dead Sea has about 35 % salt content. If you have the opportunity to swim in the Dead Sea, you will quickly learn you cannot sink. You can swim out to waters over your head, stop, reach down, pull your legs up to your chest, and just sit there. Most of the people who have traveled to the Holy Land with me were reluctant to believe this until they tried it and found it to be true. It is a weird feeling to grab hold of your knees and just sit there in the water!

The Jordan River flows into the Dead Sea, but no one has found an outlet where water leaves the Dead Sea. You would think it would be overflowing with surplus water, but instead, the Dead Sea is shrinking with every passing year. It is considerably smaller now than it was on my first trip fifty-two years ago. Places that once were a couple of minutes' walk from the water now take close to twenty minutes to be able to stick your foot in the water. Hotels built on the water's edge years ago have closed because now they are too far from the water to serve as a resort and a place where people can bask in the mineral-rich waters of the Dead Sea. There is great concern that the Dead Sea may cease to exist before too many more year's pass. Several reasons can explain why the Dead Sea is dying, but that is not the purpose of my study.

I want to propose a spiritual truth from what we literally see with our eyes of flesh. The Sea of Galilee is a freshwater sea that is full of life. The fish from the waters and the vegetation around it have fed families for as long as anyone can remember. It is a place of nourishment and the cities around it flourish because of its life-giving water.

The Dead Sea is just the opposite. It is a saltwater sea that is so salty that nothing can live in it. Even the desert area around it reeks of death. It is a hot, dry, and arid region that stands in stark contrast to the area around the Sea of Galilee which has a much more comfortable climate capable of producing an abundant harvest.

What's the difference? The most obvious is that the Sea of Galilee has water flowing in and water flowing out. This receiving and giving produces life in and around it. On the other hand, the Dead Sea has water flowing in but nothing flowing out. It receives, but it does not give. As a result, both the Sea and the land around it are dead.

The Sea of Galilee and the Dead Sea are both fed by the same source, but one is alive and the other is dead.

There is a simple yet powerful truth here that applies to our spiritual lives and life in general. For us to be the best we can be, especially the way that God desires us to be, we must be people who not only receive; we must be people who give. That kind of lifestyle not only enriches us, it also enriches and blesses those around us.

Strangely enough, the Dead Sea is rich in minerals. People from all over the world travel to cover themselves in the mud from these salty waters with hopes that it will help produce a healthier body. Once again, we see a Bible truth that is expressed in Isaiah 45:3, "God has hidden riches in secret places" with which He provides and blesses His creation.

If you ever find yourself at the Dead Sea, I hope you have time to take a swim. At the same time, however, contemplate the history of where you are. Is this close to where Sodom and Gomorrah once existed? It's a fascinating place to visit, and as I said, you will be at the lowest point on the earth.

~ Hebron And Machpelah ~

My first visit to Hebron was in 1970. I was still a teenage boy at the time. Hebron is considered by the Jews as the second holiest site in Israel, after the Temple Mount. Hebron is located twenty miles south of Jerusalem, but Jerusalem is not in the picture when we are first introduced to Hebron.

In Genesis chapter 12, due to a famine, Abraham made an ill-advised trip to Egypt that would later cause him great difficulty. The repercussions of that trip still trouble the world today. In Genesis chapter 13, when Abraham leaves Egypt, he goes back to Bethel where he had first built an altar and where God had made a promise to him. By this time, Abraham had become a man with great possessions. The same was true of his nephew Lot. Their combined flocks were so large that it was difficult to find sufficient grazing land. Lot chose to pitch his tent near Sodom while Abraham pitched his tent in Mamre, near Hebron.

It was in Hebron, some years later, where Abraham's wife Sarah died. It must have felt more like home than any of the other places Abraham had lived because he wanted to bury his wife there. Abraham had such a good reputation among those who lived in the area that they offered to give him any cave he desired. Abraham chose a cave in Machpelah, owned by a man named Ephron. The people offered to give it to him, and later Ephron offered it, but Abraham refused to take it as a gift. Genesis 23:17, "And the field of Ephron, which was in Machpelah, which was before Mamre, the field, and the cave which was therein, and all the trees that were in the field, that were in all the borders round about, were made sure."

Later, Abraham was buried there, followed by Isaac and Rebekah, and finally Jacob and Leah. Jewish tradition also says that Adam and Eve are buried here. Could that be why Abraham chose that cave? Today it is under Palestinian control and is known to Jewish inhabitants as the Tomb of the Patriarchs. Muslims refer to it as the Sanctuary of Abraham.

Hebron is mentioned in Joshua chapter 10 in connection with that famous battle where the sun stood still. In Joshua chapter 14, Caleb requested the land of Hebron for his faithful service to Moses and the part he played in helping the children of Israel take back the Promised Land. Of the twelve spies sent to search out the Promised Land, only Joshua and Caleb brought back a good report. In Numbers chapter 13, they brought a huge cluster of grapes from the "Valley of Eshcol," which was near Hebron. Joshua later named Hebron a "city of refuge." (Joshua 20) When the people from Gaza tried to kill Samson, he ripped the city gates off their hinges and carried them upon his back to a hill that overlooked Hebron.

Years later, when David became King of Judah, God told him to go to Hebron. (2 Samuel 2) Hebron became the city where David ruled for seven years and six months because the Jebusites controlled Jerusalem at that time. In 2 Samuel chapter 5, representatives from all the tribes came to Hebron and chose David to be King over all of Israel. After conquering the Jebusites, David moved his capital to Jerusalem.

Hebron held good memories for David concerning how he first became king, but years later it would become one of the saddest chapters in his life. David's son Absalom decided he wanted to be king. While putting together a plan to overthrow his father, he made Hebron his headquarters. Absalom made many mistakes during his life, but this attempted coup would be the worse. While we will never know all his thoughts, it's possible he believed that since David began his reign in Hebron while Saul was still alive, it would also work for him.

Absalom forgot a vital truth. David had been anointed by God to rule Israel; he had not. As significant as Hebron was to his ancestors, a cave full of ancestral bones could not replace the anointing.

God is still calling people to follow Him. Our challenge is to find our place in the Kingdom and serve Him with all our hearts. God honors the anointing; He does not honor a rebellious spirit.

~ Mount Sinai ~

The very mention of the name invokes feelings of awe. It was a place of divine encounter between God and man. It was a place where a set of laws were established that have influenced nations around the world who make no claim to being either Jewish or Christian. It was where God gave Moses a detailed description of how to build the Wilderness Tabernacle and everything associated with that Tabernacle, including the Holy of Holies. It is Mount Sinai.

There is controversy as to where this mountain is located. Some say it is in the Sinai Peninsula on a landmass between the Gulf of Suez and the Gulf of Aqaba, better known as the Red Sea. The places mentioned in Exodus chapters 15 through 18 immediately after the children of Israel left Egypt seem to bear this out. Josephus was partial to this location, which is also the home of a 1,700-year-old monastery known as St. Catherine's. There is a chapel in St. Catherine's known as the "Chapel of the Burning Bush." They claim this is the actual bush where Moses had his first encounter with God. (Exodus 3)

You can hike from St. Catherine's to the top of the mountain if you have a few hours to spare. You will pass by a spring on your way up, and you will also find a chapel dedicated to the Prophet Elijah. After having a divine encounter with God where he was supernaturally strengthened, Elijah traveled to Horeb, which is also referred to as "the mountain of God." (1 Kings 19:8)

Numerous places throughout the Bible refer to Mount Sinai as Mount Horeb. Exodus 3:1, "Now Moses kept the flock of Jethro his father-in-law, the priest of Midian: and he led the flock to the backside of the desert, and came to the mountain of God, even to Horeb." Along with the verse in Galatians 4:25, this scripture causes some to believe that Mount Sinai is in modern-day Saudi Arabia.

Interestingly, Moses and Elijah both had a divine encounter with God on Mount Sinai, and these same two men would later have a divine encounter with Jesus on the Mount of Transfiguration. Matthew 17:1-3, "And after six days Jesus taketh Peter, James, and John, his brother, and bringeth them up into a high mountain apart, And was transfigured before them: and His face did shine as the sun, and His raiment was white as the light. And, behold, there appeared unto them Moses and Elias talking with him."

In some ways, the New Testament encounter is reminiscent of what happened in the Old Testament. There were times when the glory of God descended upon the mountain in the form of a fiery cloud that made the mountain look as if it were on fire.

Exodus 19:16, "And it came to pass on the third day in the morning, that there were thunders and lightnings, and a thick cloud upon the mount, and the voice of the trumpet exceeding loud; so that all the people that was in the camp trembled." What was happening on the mountain was so holy, that in this same chapter, the people were instructed to not even touch the mountain when the cloud was upon it.

And yet, on top of the mountain we know that Moses would spend a total of 80 days in the presence of God. He heard the audible voice of God. He saw the fiery finger of God write on tablets of stone. When Moses came down from the mountain the second time, his face shone so brightly they had to put a veil over his face. Moses had experienced the glory of God in a manner that is unequaled in the Bible.

When I stood at the base of this mountain, I was not so much concerned with whether this was the actual location as I was with the story of what happened on a mountain somewhere in this area. To think of the relationship that God desires to have with His people is humbling and overwhelming. After Eve disobeyed God and partook of the forbidden fruit, God could have just forgotten about Adam and Eve, but God still desired to have fellowship with His creation. While the fulness of this relationship will not be realized on this earth, it will be realized in heaven. That is where I want to go; how about you?

~ Jericho ~

For most people, I would say that Jericho is remembered for two things: a wall and a tree.

Jericho claims to be the oldest city in the world. Elisha's spring is there and is still supplying water. When Jesus gave the parable of the Good Samaritan in Luke chapter 10, the Bible says, "He went down from Jerusalem to Jericho." In the most literal sense, it is talking about an elevation change. Jericho is only a few miles from the Dead Sea, the lowest point on earth, with an elevation change of about 3,700 feet from Jerusalem. You literally go down to get to Jericho.

The first mention of Jericho in the Bible is connected to a story you may miss with a casual reading. In Numbers 22:1, the children of Israel set up camp on the Jordan River, opposite Jericho. They are not yet ready to enter the Promised Land, but it won't be long. When Balak, the King of the Moabites, saw them, he was fearful. He had seen how they conquered every army they encountered, and he felt sure they would defeat him. He called for a man named Balaam to put a curse on the children of Israel. I will not go into the details of that story in this devotion, but this was the occasion when a donkey would speak, showing he had more sense than Balaam.

After Moses died and Joshua succeeded him as the leader, there came that fateful day the children of Israel had longed for. After forty years in the wilderness they are about to enter the Promised Land. Can you imagine how excited they must have been? Joshua sent two men into Jericho to secretly spy it out. They found lodging in the most unlikely place, the home of a prostitute.

Although she was living an immoral life, she seemed to have some knowledge of God and knew that God was about to do something special for His people. She wanted to be on the winning side, so she made a decision that would forever change her life. The change in her life was so dramatic that she factors into the genealogy of Jesus.

God gave Joshua a most unusual command regarding how they would win the battle and defeat Jericho. They were to march around the walls in silence once a day for six days. The priests were to walk with them, carrying the Ark of the Covenant as a sign of God's presence. On the seventh day they were to march around the city seven times. When Joshua gave the signal, the priests were to blow their trumpets, and the people would give a mighty shout. They did exactly as Joshua commanded and Jericho's walls came tumbling down.

The children of Israel were not supposed to keep any of the spoils of war for themselves, but rather "all the silver and gold and the articles of bronze and iron were consecrated to the Lord." In one sense, Jericho was a "tithe." God's people were to honor Him with the first fruits of the conquest.

In 2 Kings chapter 2, the water at Jericho had become undrinkable. God used the Prophet Elisha to "heal the waters." They are still healed today because I have tasted the waters of that fountain.

Jericho is mentioned in Mark chapter 10 when the blind beggar Bartimaeus was healed.

But the story many of us grew up hearing in Sunday School was about a wee little man named Zacchaeus.

Zacchaeus was a chief tax collector. Luke 19:1-10 tells the story of an occasion when Jesus was passing through Jericho. Somehow Zacchaeus had heard about Jesus and was determined to see him. Since he was a short man, he found a sycamore tree to climb so he would have a good view. His determination so impressed Jesus that He told Zacchaeus to come down from that tree because he wanted to eat a meal with him at his home.

The Bible tells us that Zacchaeus was rich; his riches undoubtedly gained from his tax collecting. The people hated him and considered him a vile sinner, but after meeting Jesus, Zacchaeus vowed to give half of all he owned to the poor, and if he had taken anything falsely, he would restore it fourfold. Jesus declared that salvation had come to the house of Zacchaeus. When a person truly gets saved, it will affect their pocketbook.

~ Hazor ~

Jericho was just the first of many places that had to be conquered as the children of Israel set about inheriting the land God had originally promised to Abraham. What happened at Jericho is a well-known story, but I suspect most people are not familiar with a city in the Bible named Hazor. Hazor is significant for several reasons.

As the armies of Israel began to march steadily across the land, the kings of that region realized the only hope they had for survival was to band together. We see that in Joshua chapter 11. It is in this same chapter that Hazor is first mentioned. It was an exceedingly wicked place and has the distinction of being the only city the children of Israel defeated that Joshua commanded to be burned.

Hazor would later serve as a home for Ahab and Jezebel. It was a place where all kinds of vile and sinful worship took place. But what prompted Joshua to burn it? I have been to Hazor and seen the archaeological evidence of when this city was destroyed. Among the objects they have unearthed, they have discovered signs of child sacrifice. The taking of a child's life has always been an abomination to God, whether it is after they are born, as in the case of Hazor, or as in the horrible legal murder we call abortion. Like Sodom and Gomorrah, Hazor is evidence of God's judgment.

Some years later, Hazor factors in with another well-known Bible story. As they often did, when the children of Israel found themselves either in bondage or facing an overwhelming battle, they began to cry out to God. Judges 4:1 tells us the children of Israel had fallen into sin. There was a prophetess named Deborah who was serving as their Judge. Hazor had been rebuilt and a man named Jabin was King.

Deborah prophesied to Barak, the commander of Israel's army, that God would give him the victory if he would go fight. Barak said that he would not fight unless she went with him. He would be facing Sisera, the captain of Jabin's army, who had the entire army with all their chariots and multitudes of soldiers at his disposal. Deborah told him that she would go, but as a result, the honor of the victory would not belong to him, but rather to a woman.

Just as Deborah prophesied, when the armies met, Barak defeated Sisera. Sisera escaped and fled to the home of Heber, who was a friend of Jabin. Heber's wife, Jael, however, did not share his sentiments. She sided with God's people. When Sisera asked her to hide him, she did. But once she had covered him up, she slipped back inside and drove a spike through his head, fulfilling the second part of Deborah's prophesy. The honor of the ultimate victory went to Jael instead of Barak.

In 1 Kings chapter 9, Solomon has completed building the Temple and his palace, so he sets out on additional building projects. One of them was the rebuilding of Hazor. Several characteristics of the building style of Solomon have been identified at Hazor, as well as Megiddo and Gezer, just as the Bible says. There is also evidence of stables attributed to Solomon. According to 1 Kings 4:26, Solomon had 40,000 stalls for the horses that pulled his chariots.

The legacy of Hazor is directly connected to who was in power when the city flourished. It had several evil rulers, but there were also the days of blessings and prosperity under Solomon. This is a principle we see repeated throughout the Bible. The Bible tells us in 1 Timothy 2:1-3, "I exhort therefore, that, first of all, supplications, prayers, intercessions, and giving of thanks, be made for all men; For kings, and for all that are in authority; that we may lead a quiet and peaceable life in all godliness and honesty. For this is good and acceptable in the sight of God our Savior."

History is replete with examples of how God blesses nations who follow Him, with America being a great example. However, as America continues to turn away from God and reject His holy standards, we can expect judgment unless we repent. In many ways, America is following the examples of Hazor, Sodom, and Gomorrah. Join me in praying that America will repent before it is too late.

~ Jerusalem ~

Jerusalem, the city of our God.

Before the name was changed to Jerusalem, it was known as Salem. Four times in the Bible, it is referred to with that name. Asaph mentioned it in Psalms 76:1-2, "In Judah is God known: His name is great in Israel. In Salem also is His tabernacle, and His dwelling place in Zion." The first, and most intriguing reference to me, is found in Genesis 14:18. Abraham has just freed his nephew Lot, who had been captured in a war that involved Sodom and Gomorrah, when he meets one of the most interesting men in the Bible. "And Melchizedek King of Salem brought forth bread and wine: and he was the priest of the most high God."

The two remaining references to "Salem" are found in the Book of Hebrews, and they refer to this event in Genesis chapter 14. Who was Melchizedek? I did a series of devotions on him earlier, so I will not go into great detail in this study, except to give you something to ponder if you've not already studied him. Hebrews 7:1-4, "For this Melchisedec, King of Salem, priest of the most high God, who met Abraham returning from the slaughter of the kings, and blessed him; To whom also Abraham gave a tenth part of all; first being by interpretation King of righteousness, and after that also King of Salem, which is, King of peace; Without father, without mother, without descent, having neither beginning of days, nor end of life; but made like unto the Son of God; abideth a priest continually. Now consider how great this man was, unto whom even the patriarch Abraham gave the tenth of the spoils."

We are not only left with the mind-boggling statement, "without father, without mother, without descent, having neither beginning of days, nor end of life; but made like unto the Son of God," but we see in both references that Abraham paid tithes to him. This is the first record of someone paying tithes, and I would also add that if you read the Genesis account carefully, you will see that it is the first time communion was served. While the Bible does not mention it, you can't help but wonder if Abraham and Melchizedek met again when Abraham went to Mount Moriah to offer his son Isaac as a sacrifice, but God intervened and "offered Himself a sacrifice." Mount Moriah is in Salem, or Jerusalem.

Melchizedek's city was called Salem, or Shalem, which means the God whose worship was centered in the city. The full name was, "God Most High, Creator of Heaven and Earth," as we see in Genesis 14. It is interesting to note that after meeting Melchizedek, Abraham acknowledged this in Genesis 14:22-23 when he uses the word YHWH, the name of the covenant God of Israel. "Abram said to the king of Sodom, "I have raised my hand to the Lord (YHWH), God Most High, Creator of heaven and earth, and have taken an oath that I will accept nothing belonging to you."

The word "yeru" means "foundation stone" or "cornerstone." The name "Yeurshalem" then means "the foundation stone of God Most High, Creator of heaven and earth." Jerusalem can be said to be the cornerstone laid by the Creator of the Universe when He built the earth. There is a monument inside the Church of the Holy Sepulcher that claims to be the center of the earth.

Joshua chapter 10 is where we see the more familiar name of Jerusalem for the first time. The King of Jerusalem at that time was a man named, Adonizedek, who was possibly a descendant of Melchizedek. Notice the spelling: Melchi-zedek, Adoni-zedek.

After Joshua's death, the men of Judah attacked and captured Jerusalem and burned it. (Judges 1) Jebusites resettled the city of Jerusalem, and the city was named Jebus by its inhabitants. By David's day, the Jebusites had built walls around their city. When David was 37 years old, his men entered the city of Jerusalem through the water system and took it from the Jebusites. (2 Samuel 5:4-9)

Jerusalem, the foundation stone of the Most High God, Creator of heaven and earth, is still the center of the world's attention today. One day, there will be a new heaven, a new earth, and a new Jerusalem.

~ En Gedi ~

Ein Gedi is a beautiful place to visit. As you walk the path up to a waterfall, and then a little further to a cave that it is known for, your mind is carried back to a turbulent time in the history of the Children of Israel.

It began when God's chosen people decided they wanted to be like all the nations around them. Up until this time they did not have a king; they received their leadership from Judges and Prophets who spoke to them on behalf of God. God was their king. But when the children of Israel saw that everyone else had a king, they wanted one. The Prophet Samuel took it as a rejection of his leadership, but God told him in 1 Samuel 8:7, "they have not rejected thee, but they have rejected Me, that I should not reign over them."

Samuel tried to warn them of the consequences of what they were demanding, but they would not be denied. He put it plainly in 1 Samuel 10:19, "And ye have this day rejected your God, who Himself saved you out of all your adversities and your tribulations; and ye have said unto him, Nay, but set a king over us."

Saul was chosen as their first king and things seemed to be going okay for a while, but then something tragic happened in the heart of Saul. After winning some key battles, he allowed a spirit of pride and rebellion to enter his heart. As a result, Saul rejected the commandment of God. When Samuel found Saul, he told him in 1 Samuel 13:14, "But now thy kingdom shall not continue: the Lord hath sought a man after His own heart, and the Lord hath commanded him to be captain over His people, because thou hast not kept that which the Lord commanded thee." The man who would have a heart after God was a young shepherd boy named David.

In 1 Samuel 16:1, God tells Samuel to quit mourning over Saul, and then God sends him to Bethlehem to the home of Jesse, where he anoints David. In 1 Samuel 16:13, we see the Spirit of the Lord coming upon David and in the very next verse we see the Spirit of the Lord departing from Saul. As a result, an evil spirit began to trouble Saul's soul.

To help their king, Saul's servants recommended that a person gifted with music be sought out so he could play something that would soothe the king's heart. The person they found was none other than David. 1 Samuel 16:21, "And David came to Saul, and stood before him: and he (Saul) loved him (David) greatly, and he became his armourbearer."

This means that Saul knew David before the encounter with Goliath, but when David defeated Goliath, he came to the forefront of all the children of Israel. Saul and his army were afraid to fight this giant. David famously asked in 1 Samuel 17:29, "Is there not a cause?" After defeating Goliath, David quickly became more loved by the people than Saul. The evil spirit in Saul, combined with his jealousy over the way the people loved David, caused Saul to hate David and he set out to kill him.

In 1 Samuel chapter 24, Saul hears that David is in the region of Ein Gedi, and he sets out to kill him. Unknown to Saul, he goes into a cave where David and his men are hiding. It was the perfect opportunity for David to kill Saul, but he refused to do so. David recognized something I suspect we need to be more mindful of in our day. Although the Spirit of the Lord had departed from Saul, David remembered there was a time when he was God's anointed, and for that reason, he would not kill him. David was even sorrowful that he had cut off a portion of Saul's robe.

In 1 Chronicles chapter 16, David and the children of Israel are celebrating the return of the Ark of the Covenant to Jerusalem. David sang a Psalm to the people that is repeated in Psalms 115. In that Psalm, he uses the expression, "touch not Mine anointed, and do My prophets no harm." We live in a day when so much false doctrine is being taught. How do we respond to people who were once anointed, but have clearly walked away from the truths of God's Word? The Bible is filled with examples of Prophets who stood against those who were leading people astray. Jesus Himself did this, but the intent was always to turn them back to the truth, never to destroy them. May God help us have that same tender heart and remember, there but by the grace of God go I.

~ Beit She'an ~

Although not widely known, Beit She'an is mentioned several times in the Old Testament. The fall of King Saul to the Philistines at Gilboa is connected to this city.

1 Samuel 31:8-13, "And it came to pass on the morrow, when the Philistines came to strip the slain, that they found Saul and his three sons fallen in mount Gilboa. And they cut off his head, and stripped off his armour, and sent into the land of the Philistines round about, to publish it in the house of their idols, and among the people. And they put his armour in the house of Ashtaroth: and they fastened his body to the wall of Bethshan. (Beit She'an) And when the inhabitants of Jabeshgilead heard of that which the Philistines had done to Saul; All the valiant men arose, and went all night, and took the body of Saul and the bodies of his sons from the wall of Bethshan, and came to Jabesh, and burnt them there. And they took their bones, and buried them under a tree at Jabesh, and fasted seven days."

This story is both tragic and heroic. Beit She'an was part of the territory initially given to the tribe of Manasseh. (Joshua 17:11) But Judges 1:27 adds this, "Neither did Manasseh drive out the inhabitants of Bethshean and her towns."

Saul began his reign as the first King of Israel with such hope and promise, but his arrogance and rebellion against God's commandments caused him to lose his kingdom, and his relationship with God was severed as well. After being killed in battle, the Philistines cut his head off and nailed his body to the walls in Beit She'an. It was a humiliating defeat for the children of Israel.

Although the Philistines had just defeated the army of Israel, with their King being beheaded and his body nailed to a wall, a group of brave men from Jabeshgilead traveled all night to recover the body of their King. They did this because they remembered something Saul had done for them that prevented the right eye of all the men of Jabeshgilead from being plucked out. (1 Samuel 11)

During the 400 years of silence between the Old and the New Testament, the Greco-Roman city of Scythopolis was founded in 250 B.C., encompassing the area of ancient Beit She'an. By New Testament times, Scythopolis was the capital of Decapolis. Decapolis is referenced in several passages concerning the ministry of Jesus.

Matthew 4:24-25, "And His fame went throughout all Syria: and they brought unto Him all sick people that were taken with divers diseases and torments, and those which were possessed with devils, and those which were lunatic, and those that had the palsy; and He healed them. And there followed Him great multitudes of people from Galilee, and from Decapolis, and from Jerusalem, and from Judaea, and from beyond Jordan."

Decapolis, or Beit She'an, became the mission field for a most unlikely missionary. We read his story in Mark 5:18-20, "And when He was come into the ship, he that had been possessed with the devil prayed Him that he might be with Him. Howbeit Jesus suffered him not, but saith unto him, Go home to thy friends, and tell them how great things the Lord hath done for thee, and hath had compassion on thee. And he departed and began to publish in Decapolis how great things Jesus had done for him: and all men did marvel." These verses contain the story of Legion, the demon-possessed man from Gadara. Did you notice that once Legion had been delivered from the demons he wanted to stay with Jesus, but Jesus sent him as a missionary to Decapolis?

At the time of the Great Revolt against Rome (66-73 A.D.), many Jewish cities rebelled against their Roman rulers, but the Jewish residents of Scythopolis decided they could trust their non-Jewish neighbors. They remained unarmed and as a result were unfortunately massacred at the hands of their neighbors. A massive earthquake destroyed the entire city in October of 749 A.D. Although the ruins of this city are Roman, when I walk these streets, I can't help but be reminded of Saul, and Legion.

~ Dan ~

Most Bible readers are familiar with the expression, "from Dan to Beersheba," but they probably know little about the actual city. The history of the city of Dan seems to parallel what were possibly the last words Jacob spoke to his son Dan. Knowing he would soon die; Jacob called his sons together and spoke prophetically over them. His words to Dan were, "Dan shall be a serpent by the way, an adder in the path, that biteth the horse heels, so that his rider shall fall backward." (Genesis 49:17) These words seem to have indeed been fulfilled in the descendants of Dan and for the city that bears his name.

In Judges 18, we have an interesting story. The chapter begins by saying, "In those days, there was no king in Israel." You get the sense from those opening words that what happens next will not be good, and it wasn't. Five men from the tribe of Dan were sent to spy out the land. They would later be joined by six hundred men of war, also from the tribe of Dan. One day, the five men came across a Levite who was serving as the priest for a man named Micah. Micah had set up his own place of worship with a graven image he had made himself. The children of Dan wanted a priest of their own and a god to worship, so they asked this Levite to come with them. They asked him a question in Judges 18:19, "is it better for thee to be a priest unto the house of one man, or that thou be a priest unto a tribe and a family in Israel?" Thinking it would be more profitable for him to be the priest over an entire tribe, rather than just one man's home, he goes with them. The men from Dan proceed to take the graven image and the other instruments of worship that were in Micah's home. When Micah learns what happened, he calls his neighbors, and they pursue the children of Dan.

When they catch up with them, the six hundred men of war have joined them and Micah realizes he is outnumbered. He nonetheless pleads with them to return what they had taken. Judges 18:24, "Ye have taken away my gods which I made, and the priest, and ye are gone away: and what have I more?" They had taken his priest, who sold himself to the highest bidder, and they stole the gods he had made with his own hands.

These descendants of Dan then conquered a city named Laish and renamed it Dan, Jacob's son, from whom they were descended. They began worshipping the god they had just stolen while the rest of the children of Israel continued to worship Yahweh in Shiloh, where the Ark of the Covenant was.

This pattern of idolatry would repeat itself many years later. After Solomon dies, his son Rehoboam becomes king. Rather than heeding the wisdom of his elder counselors, he instead follows the advice of the younger men he had grown up with. A man named Jeroboam led a rebellion that resulted in the nation being divided into the southern kingdom known as Judah, and the northern kingdom known as Israel. They have never been fully reunited from the time this division occurred.

Since the temple Solomon built was in Jerusalem, the people of Judah continued to worship there. Jeroboam feared someone would kill him and the people would return to worshipping in Jerusalem, so he devised a plan. It is found in 1 Kings 12:28-30, "Whereupon the king (Jeroboam) took counsel, and made two calves of gold, and said unto them, It is too much for you to go up to Jerusalem: behold thy gods, O Israel, which brought thee up out of the land of Egypt. And he set the one in Bethel, and the other put he in Dan. And this thing became a sin: for the people went to worship before the one, even unto Dan."

Incredibly, the ten tribes began to worship a golden calf like the one the children of Israel made when they first left Egypt. Just as their ancestors had done, they dared say this was the god who delivered them from Egyptian bondage. The children of Israel worshipped a god that Aaron made with his own hands, Micah worshipped a god he made with his own hands, and now the ten tribes of Israel were worshipping a god that Jeroboam made with his own hands. The latter instance was in the city of Dan, which was what Jeroboam intended to be a substitute for Jerusalem.

The ruins of the city of Dan are impressive, but sadly its history is filled with tragic rebellion and unbelief.

~ Mount Carmel ~

It only takes 63 words for the fire to fall. 1 Kings 18:37-38, "Lord God of Abraham, Isaac, and of Israel, let it be known this day that Thou art God in Israel, and that I am thy servant, and that I have done all these things at Thy word. Hear me, O Lord, hear me, that these people may know that Thou art the Lord God, and that Thou hast turned their heart back again. Then the fire of the Lord fell."

Mount Carmel was where the Prophet Elijah had an encounter with the 450 prophets of Baal and the 400 prophets of the grove. The prophets of the grove worshipped Asherah, who was known by various names, but the root of her worship goes back to Babylon and the goddess Ishtar.

The encounter in 1 Kings chapter 18 actually began in chapter 17. Because Ahab and Jezebel were such wicked rulers, Elijah prophesied in verse 1 that there would not be any dew or rain until he said so. Three years later, Elijah, Ahab, Jezebel, and all the false prophets meet on top of Carmel in a dramatic confrontation.

Elijah challenged the false prophets to a demonstration of who was able to visibly accept a sacrificial offering. It would be the God who answered by fire. After preparing their altar, these pagan prophets spent all day trying to get their god to hear and accept their offering, but to no avail.

Then Elijah steps up. He repaired the altar using twelve stones, representing the twelve tribes of Israel. After placing the sacrifice on the altar, he does a most unusual thing. He pours twelve barrels of water over the sacrifice, drenching everything to the point that water runs over the trench around the altar. The sacrifice and wood were soaked with water.

The most obvious conclusion is that this would make it even harder for God to set this altar on fire. But there is something greater happening here. Remember, it had not rained for three years. Water had become extremely valuable. We know the brook Cherith where Elijah stayed for some time had dried up. Pouring water on the sacrifice not only made it more difficult to burn, it also increased the value of the sacrifice. Water was a precious commodity.

After Elijah's 63-word prayer, God did, in fact, answer by fire. 1 Kings 18:38, "Then the fire of the Lord fell and consumed the burnt sacrifice, and the wood, and the stones, and the dust, and licked up the water that was in the trench." As a result, the people turned back to God. In verse 41 of this same chapter, Elijah prophesied to Ahab, "I hear the sound of the abundance of rain."

Many lessons can be learned from the events surrounding this story but let me mention just one. God is moved by the sincere prayer of His people. There was nothing fancy or elaborate about Elijah's prayer; it just came from the heart of a faithful follower. Some prayers touch the throne of God, while others are just sounding brass and tinkling cymbals.

Through the years, numerous people commented about the prayers my Daddy used to pray. If you ever heard Daddy pray, you know they were not the average prayer. There was a divine connection when Daddy prayed, and all in attendance could sense that. That's how it should be.

Jesus addressed the importance of sincere prayers, versus people who pray at length just to be noticed. Mark 12:38-40, "Beware of the scribes, which love to go in long clothing, and love salutations in the marketplaces, And the chief seats in the synagogues, and the uppermost rooms at feasts: Which devour widows' houses, and for a pretense make long prayers."

In the case of the 850 false prophets that Elijah confronted on Mount Carmel, they prayed all day, cutting themselves, jumping up and down, and probably several other things, hoping their god would wake up and answer by fire. Their chiseled god of stone could not respond, but with a simple 63-word prayer, the One True God was moved to respond. He is still answering prayers today.

~ Babylon ~

In a previous devotion, I dealt with the Tower of Babel. It is impossible to completely separate the issues of that story from this devotion because that was the birthplace of Babylon. But in this devotion I want to look at the ongoing encounters between Babylon and the children of Israel and then touch briefly on the prophetic parts yet to be fulfilled.

Babylon is first mentioned in Joshua chapter 7. The children of Israel had just defeated Jericho and confidently moved to fight their next opponent. The battle at Ai should have been a simple matter, yet the children of Israel were defeated. Was it arrogance and pride that caused their defeat? No, it was an act of disobedience at Jericho that caused this humiliating defeat. Silver and gold, along with a beautiful garment made in Babylon, drove a man named Achan to disobey the command of God. Babylon was already indirectly causing trouble.

Many years would pass before Babylon would be mentioned in the Bible again. When Rehoboam became the fourth King of the nation of Israel, the nation suffered a division that has never been reconciled. In 2 Kings chapter 17, the Bible tells us the northern Kingdom of Israel was living in sin, and the southern Kingdom of Judah was also. For the first time in the Bible, we see an invading army comprised partly of soldiers from Babylon.

In 2 Kings chapter 25, Nebuchadnezzar, King of Babylon, laid siege to Jerusalem for eighteen months and eventually conquered it. Solomon's Temple was destroyed during this conflict. Intending to obliterate Jerusalem completely, Nebuchadnezzar even tore down the walls.

Many people were carried into Babylonian captivity as a result of this invasion, including Daniel, Shadrach, Meshach, and Abednego. Each of these four men would face an extreme moment in their life when they had to choose whether or not they would stand for the One True God.

In Daniel's case, he had to decide if he would continue to pray to God as was his custom, or if he would submit to a law specifically targeted at him. He chose to continue to worship God as he always had, and God delivered him from the mouth of the lions. (Daniel 6)

In Daniel chapter 3, Shadrach, Meshach, and Abednego were faced with a decision as to whether or not they would bow down and worship a 90-foot-tall golden image that Nebuchadnezzar had made, apparently of himself. It seems to have been a reaction to the interpretation of Nebuchadnezzar's dream in chapter 2. Everyone else bowed, but the three Hebrew boys would not. It caused them to be cast into a fiery furnace, but a fourth Man was in that furnace with them. Nebuchadnezzar correctly identified Him as "the Son of God." Jesus walked into the midst of the fire with them, and Shadrach, Meshach, and Abednego came out without so much as the smell of smoke on their garments.

It is the prophetic connections to Babylon however, that has everyone fascinated today. Babylon is mentioned in the Book of Revelation as having two separate and distinct meanings. First, Babylon the Great is a literal city. Will this future city be in Iraq where the first Babylon was built? Saddam Hussein started rebuilding Babylon before he was killed, believing he was a reincarnated

Nebuchadnezzar. Will someone complete that city or will it be somewhere else, like Rome perhaps?

Mystery Babylon on the other hand is a religious system; it is the religion of the Antichrist. It will be a religion steeped in the same form of worship that began at the Tower of Babel. After the languages were confused, this religion was spread all over the world. That's why you find so many identical forms of worship, albeit with different names for their deities, in numerous cultures with no common connection, except for Babylon.

What we see is simply this. The rebellion in Babylon was the same demonic rebellion that began at some point in the dateless past when Lucifer dared believe he could overthrow God. Although he was cast out of heaven, he is still trying to dethrone God. We know the end of the story and his final defeat. The question that everyone is asking is this, "how long, oh Lord?"

~ Assyria ~

Assyria is first mentioned in Genesis chapter 2 as the location through which the Hiddekel River flowed from the Garden of Eden. In our devotion on Mount Ararat, I mentioned a group of people who lived in that area known as the Kingdom of Urartu or the Kingdom of Van, who often found themselves involved in warfare with Assyria. This constant battling probably played a part in people moving further south into the area where the Tower of Babel would later be built.

The Assyrians were often the enemies of the children of Israel. In 2 Kings chapter 18, the Assyrian King Sennacherib attacked Jerusalem. In an attempt to get Hezekiah to surrender, Sennacherib tells Hezekiah that he has defeated several other nations, and their gods were powerless to stop him. He then takes it a step further and says that Hezekiah's God would also be powerless. Hezekiah rent his clothes and went to the house of the Lord and cried out, "did you hear what this heathen king said? He said that not even You can deliver us."

Hezekiah sent messengers to the Prophet Isaiah to inform him what was happening. Isaiah told Hezekiah that he should not worry because God had heard his prayer and Sennacherib would not be successful. The words of the Prophet encouraged Hezekiah. He called the people together and spoke these words of encouragement in 2 Chronicles 32:7-8, "Be strong and courageous, be not afraid nor dismayed for the king of Assyria, nor for all the multitude that is with him: for there be more with us than with him. With him is an arm of flesh; but with us is the Lord our God to help us, and to fight our battles. And the people rested themselves upon the words of Hezekiah king of Judah."

Sennacherib tried to frighten the people into surrendering, but Isaiah and Hezekiah began to cry out to God. God dispatched an angel, and the next morning Sennacherib woke up to find that 185,000 of his soldiers were dead. Humiliated, he goes home where he is killed by two of his sons.

Zephaniah prophesied the destruction of Assyria. Zephaniah 2:13, "And He will stretch out His hand against the north and destroy Assyria; and will make Nineveh a desolation, and dry like a wilderness." The destruction of Nineveh was so complete by the Medes and the Babylonians that its ruins would not be discovered for hundreds of years.

Nineveh, the ancient capital of Assyria, was such a wicked place that God decided to destroy it, but not before giving them an opportunity to repent. Jonah most likely did not want to go to Nineveh because of the hatred the children of Israel had for the way the Assyrians had treated them through the years. He feared they would repent, and that God would spare them. Jonah did not want God to spare them; he wanted God to destroy them. But as you know, they did repent, and at this particular time they were spared. It proves yet again that God is not willing that any should perish, that all should come to repentance. I wish we could all be convinced of how much God loves the world.

Having said that, we must not forget that Assyria is just one example of a nation which thought they were invincible. Although they were a great world power at one time, they are now relegated to the dusty pages of history. I believe God raised up America for such a time as this, but America is turning its back on God and unless America repents, we will not be spared God's judgment. We are trampling the truths of God's Word under our feet every day, and just like the nations before us, we will not be spared unless we turn from our wicked ways and repent.

~ Nazareth ~

We have left the pages of the Old Testament behind us. Some may wonder why I mentioned Egypt, Assyria, and Babylon, but neglected to mention Greece and Rome. While Greece and Rome were two of the greatest world powers to ever exist, their influence is felt more in the stories of the New Testament, Rome in particular. I will touch on these nations as we proceed through our study.

Nazareth was a small village 2,000 years ago, with a population of about 300, so everyone knew everyone else. It did not have a good reputation as evidenced by Nathaniel's question in John 1:46, "can anything good come out of Nazareth?" And yet, in this small insignificant village, God sent an angel to a young girl named Mary.

Nazareth is not even mentioned in the Old Testament. The first time it shows up on the pages of the Bible is when the angel Gabriel makes an announcement that would forever change the world. The long-awaited Messiah was about to be born. It's interesting that although Jesus was born in Bethlehem, just as the Prophets had foretold in Micah 5:2, He is frequently referred to as Jesus of Nazareth. Nazareth was the village where He grew up, but the fact that it became so attached to the Son of God shows that God looks at things differently than we do.

If man had planned the birth of the Messiah, they would have almost certainly chosen the capital of Rome and had Jesus born into a wealthy family. Instead, God chose a town with a less than desirable reputation and allowed Jesus to be raised by people who were poor. We know they were poor by what they offered as a sacrifice at the Temple when Jesus was dedicated. (Luke 2:24)

Jesus chose Nazareth as the place where He read the prophecy of Isaiah chapter 61 that spoke of the coming Messiah. Luke elaborated on that occasion in chapter 4. When Jesus finished reading, He declared that He was the fulfillment of this prophecy. You would think they would have been deliriously happy, but instead, they tried to kill Him. His hometown had rejected Him. The ones who had watched Him grow up could not see anything beyond the son of a carpenter, when in truth, He was the long-awaited Son of God. From that point forward, Jesus moved what we would call His headquarters to the city of Capernaum.

I always enjoy my visits to Nazareth. The Church of the Annunciation is built over the place they say is the home of Mary, where the angel Gabriel appeared to her. Nearby is a place called Nazareth Village. As you walk through this recreated village, you can see what Nazareth would have looked like 2,000 years ago. They even have a carpenter named Joseph. Archaeologists have uncovered ruins of ancient Nazareth that date back to the time of Christ. The one place you can visit that is almost certainly authentic is a well, known as Mary's Well. You can close your eyes and almost see her walking there daily to get water.

It is a fascinating place to visit, but you miss the true meaning of what happened in Nazareth if you don't pause and reflect on God's promise to Adam and Eve in Genesis chapter 3. That promise, along with all the prophecies of the Old Testament, was fulfilled with the birth of a Savior.

Some who are reading these words may have been born into a home of wealth and affluence. Most of us were not, but each of us can take comfort knowing that God can use us regardless of where we came from. He doesn't overlook what the world considers small and insignificant. God is looking for a willing vessel through whom He can bless the world. Little is much when God is in it.

~ Bethlehem ~

Close your eyes for a moment and imagine the sky filled with a multitude of the heavenly host, and listen as an angel declares, "unto you is born this day in the city of David, a Savior which is Christ the Lord." (Luke 2:11)

The Shepherd's Field is a favorite place to visit in Bethlehem. Numerous caves dot the landscape. It has long been known as an area where shepherds tend their flocks. Some caves have been converted into places where groups can go inside and have devotions. When I'm there, I always take time to walk to the side of the hill that overlooks a beautiful valley. As I gaze across the valley to a mountain in the distance, an incredible panoramic view of the area unfolds. When I stand there, I do exactly what I suggested you do when I began this devotion. I close my eyes and imagine what it was like on that fateful night when the angel gave those shepherds the greatest news they would ever hear; "a Savior has been born."

Bethlehem has quite an ancient history, being first mentioned in Genesis chapter 35. While on a journey, Rachel goes into labor and gives birth to a son, Benjamin. Unfortunately, she dies giving birth and Jacob buries his beloved wife in Bethlehem. I have been by the tomb numerous times and you can't help but remember all that happened when Jacob and Rachel married. There is a touch of sadness to the story. Jacob loved Rachel, but on his wedding night, he learned he had been given her sister Leah to be his wife instead. He worked a total of fourteen years for the one he loved. In death, they were also separated. Rather than being buried beside her husband in Machpelah, that honor also fell to her sister, leaving Rachael to be buried all alone in Bethlehem.

While Bethlehem is mentioned several times throughout the Old Testament, let me briefly point out just three. In the Book of Ruth, we have the story of Elimelech and his wife Naomi. Due to a famine, they left Bethlehem, which ironically means "house of bread," and moved to Moab. Tragedy struck their family while there. Elimelech and both of Naomi's sons died. Naomi decided to return home. Her two daughters-in-law had a decision to make. Would they stay in their homeland or would they go with Naomi? Orpah chose to stay in Moab, but Ruth famously said, "Intreat me not to leave thee, or to return from following after thee: for whither thou goest, I will go; and where thou lodgest, I will lodge: thy people shall be my people, and thy God my God: Where thou diest, will I die, and there will I be buried: the Lord do so to me, and more also, if ought but death part thee and me." (Ruth 1:16-17) It proved to be a fateful decision because Boaz became her kinsman-redeemer, thus putting Ruth in the lineage of Jesus. She was King David's great-grandmother.

Apparently, the family stayed in that area, leading to the second event I will mention briefly. When the Prophet Samuel went looking for someone to anoint as king to replace Saul, God directed him to Bethlehem, where he found a young shepherd boy. The hometown of David would be the reason why Joseph and Mary had to make a journey many years later.

The third Old Testament reference is found in Micah 5:2, "But thou, Bethlehem Ephratah, though thou be little among the thousands of Judah, yet out of thee shall He come forth unto me that is to be ruler in Israel; whose goings forth have been from of old, from everlasting."

Interestingly, the next time Bethlehem is mentioned in the Bible is in the New Testament, when the words of the Prophet are fulfilled. "And Joseph also went up from Galilee, out of the city of Nazareth, into Judaea, unto the city of David, which is called Bethlehem; (because he was of the house and lineage of David:) To be taxed with Mary his espoused wife, being great with child. And so it was, that, while they were there, the days were accomplished that she should be delivered. And she brought forth her firstborn son, and wrapped Him in swaddling clothes, and laid Him in a manger; because there was no room for them in the inn." (Luke 2:4-7)

On a sentimental note, the mention of Bethlehem stirs up a beautiful memory. When I was a boy, every year at Christmas, the church where my Dad was pastor had a Christmas program. My Mom and Sister Pearl Finch would always sing, *"O Beautiful Star Of Bethlehem."* Whenever I hear that song, my thoughts immediately flashback to those days.

~ The Jordan River ~

There are many well-known rivers around the world, but none more famous than the Jordan River. It's not very long compared to other great rivers, being only a little over 150 miles in length, but it stands out because of the significance of what happened in and around this river.

We are first introduced to Jordan in Genesis chapter 13 when Lot chose the "well-watered plains of the Jordan." He decided to move there because it was appealing to the eye, ignoring the great wickedness of Sodom and Gomorrah in the process. The first reference to the river itself is in Genesis chapter 32, when Jacob is about to be reunited with his brother Esau.

Numerous references to events either on this side of Jordan, or the other side of the Jordan, are mentioned right up to the point when the children of Israel are about to enter the Promised Land. The long-awaited return home is immediately met with two obstacles. Before they could even get to the great walled city of Jericho, the flooded waters of the Jordan River stood in their way.

Two tremendous miracles stand as bookends to the children of Israel leaving Egypt and entering the Promised Land. In the case of the Red Sea, God parted the waters. In the case of the Jordan River, God chose to stop the water from flowing, causing them to back up many miles. One can only imagine what an incredible sight that would have been.

In Joshua chapter 3, when the command was given to begin the march, the waters were still flowing until the feet of the priests touched the water. How would you feel if you were headed into raging floodwaters carrying the Ark of the Covenant, with only the hope that something miraculous would happen? That's truly a step of faith. And yet, that is exactly what they did, and that is exactly what happened. God made a way when there seemed to be no way. What appeared to be an obstacle became a highway of deliverance instead.

The Jordan River is well-known for a baptismal service. As God is bringing all things to pass regarding the promise He made in Genesis chapter 3, He sends a man to prepare the way for the Messiah. His name was John. Born with a specific call upon his life, John comes with a message. The first word the Bible records him saying was, "repent." (Matthew 3:2) He came to point people to Jesus.

There is evidence near Ein Karem, the hometown of John, that he baptized people in places other than the Jordan River. On one of my trips, our group had the opportunity to become amateur archaeologists for three days. We dug at a site known as *"The Cave of John the Baptist."* Shimon Gibson was the lead archaeologist excavating this cave and would later write a book about it. He was with us one day during our dig. There is evidence that John actually baptized people in this cave.

Of all the many baptisms that John performed, the greatest is recorded in all four of the Gospel letters. One day a Man comes to be baptized that John immediately recognized as "the Lamb of God, who takes away the sin of the world." (John 1:29) Forty days later when Jesus came out of the wilderness, after a time of fasting and temptation, the first word that Jesus spoke was, "repent." "From that time Jesus began to preach, and to say,

Repent: for the kingdom of heaven is at hand." (Matthew 4:17)

I fear we have complicated the Gospel. The simplicity of the Gospel is that God loves us, Jesus died for our sins, and if we want to spend eternity in heaven, we must repent. We are very much like the Pharisees of old in that we have added a lot of man-made traditions. If we are not extremely careful, we are pressured to please man more than God.

The Jordan River stands as a place of the miraculous, and it also stands as a place of obedience. Jesus set the example for us to follow. We should never be ashamed to make a public stand for our Savior. We need to proudly proclaim to the world that I am a Christian. The old me has been buried beneath the water, and a new creation in Christ has come forth from a watery grave. Every chance we get, we need to "tell somebody about Jesus."

The Land Of The Bible

~ The Sea Of Galilee ~

The Sea of Galilee is not really a sea; it is a lake. Luke mentions it five times in his writing, but with a different name. Luke 5:1, "And it came to pass, that, as the people pressed upon Him to hear the word of God, He stood by the Lake of Gennesaret." Gennesaret was an area on the northwest coast of the Sea of Galilee, whose land was rich and fertile. The Book of Revelation is the only other place in the New Testament where the word "lake" is used. It is also used five times, but there it is speaking about "a lake of fire."

Matthew and Mark mention the Sea of Galilee, but John throws in a third name. John 6:1, "After these things Jesus went over the Sea of Galilee, which is the Sea of Tiberias." Whatever name you know it by, it is held in such high esteem that the label of being a "sea" is forever attached to it.

On one of my trips several years ago, I learned something that had somehow eluded my attention, although I have read through the Bible many times. I learned that over 85% of Jesus' ministry took place around and on the Sea of Galilee. From that perspective, this area could rightly be called the "cradle of the Gospel." Of the thirty-seven miracles recorded in the Bible from the earthly ministry of Jesus, twenty-five took place in Galilee. Of course, countless thousands are not recorded. Matthew 15:30, "And great multitudes came unto Him, having with them those that were lame, blind, dumb, maimed, and many others, and cast them down at Jesus' feet; and He healed them." Luke, the physician, said in Luke 4:40, "Now when the sun was setting, all they that had any sick with divers diseases brought them unto Him; and He laid His hands on every one of them, and healed them." One can only imagine how many experienced the miracle-working power of the Son of God in this area.

Jesus called His first disciples at the Sea of Galilee. Matthew 4:18-22, "And Jesus, walking by the sea of Galilee, saw two brethren, Simon called Peter, and Andrew his brother, casting a net into the sea: for they were fishers. And He saith unto them, Follow Me, and I will make you fishers of men. And they straightway left their nets and followed Him. And going on from thence, He saw other two brethren, James the son of Zebedee, and John, his brother, in a ship with Zebedee, their father, mending their nets; and He called them. And they immediately left the ship and their father and followed Him."

In Mark chapter 4, we have the story of Jesus and His disciples heading across the Sea of Galilee when a storm arose. Several of the disciples were experienced fishermen and had undoubtedly seen many storms on the sea, but this storm was so fierce they feared for their life. Meanwhile, Jesus is taking a nap in the back part of the boat. Thinking they were about to die; they woke Him up. When He saw their fear, and the storm, He simply said, "Peace, be still." I have always looked at that verse like this. The first word Jesus spoke was directed to His disciples. They were afraid and they needed peace. So, the word "peace," was for them. The words "be still," were directed to the storm. When Jesus spoke, the storm had to lay down and be calm because it recognized the voice of the Master. I'm glad Jesus is still the peace speaker to the storms of our life.

And then, of course, there was the time when Jesus defied all the laws of nature and walked on water. To fully understand this, I would suggest a thorough study of Matthew chapter 14. I will only touch on the highlights. In verse 12, Jesus learns that John the Baptist has been killed. In verse 14, Jesus healed a multitude of people. Over the following several verses, Jesus fed 5,000 men, not counting the women and children. As the day draws to a close, He sends His Disciples across the Sea of Galilee, telling them that He will join them later. He is exhausted, and He needs to spend time in prayer.

While on the mountaintop, He sees His disciples caught in another storm on the sea. They need Him again, so Jesus comes down from the mountain, and when He gets to water He just keeps walking. There may or may not have been a boat there that He could have used, but He decided that a boat was not necessary. As Peter would learn a few minutes later, miracles happen when we dare to take a step of faith.

~ Capernaum ~

Throughout the New Testament, Jesus is referred to as "Jesus of Nazareth." This is understandable since Nazareth was where the angel Gabriel appeared to Mary, and it was where Joseph, Mary, and Jesus returned after His birth. Nazareth was His hometown. As we discussed in a previous devotion, when Jesus began His ministry following His baptism in the Jordan River by John the Baptist, and after spending forty days in the wilderness, Jesus returned to Nazareth and spoke in the synagogue. The Scripture He read from Isaiah clearly identified Him as the long-awaited Messiah. But rather than accept Jesus as the One they had been looking for, they rejected Him and tried to kill him.

While Matthew chapter 4 does not give as much information about this incident as Luke chapter 4 does, we see that when Jesus is essentially rejected and driven out of Nazareth, He goes to Capernaum, which will serve as His headquarters for the next three years. Matthew 9:1 calls Capernaum "His own city." Capernaum sits on the northwest shore of the Sea of Galilee and is an impressive place to visit. A two-minute walk can have you on a boat where you can sail to any of the places around the Sea of Galilee. This allowed Jesus to easily minister in the many places we read about in the Gospel accounts of His ministry.

Capernaum was where Peter, Andrew, James, John, and possibly Matthew all lived, and it was in this area where Jesus called them to follow Him. Numerous miracles occurred here. Peter's mother-in-law was healed, and money was found in the mouth of a fish which was used to pay their taxes. Jairus's daughter was raised from the dead, and the woman with the issue of blood was healed. While teaching in the synagogue one Sabbath, a demon-possessed man tried to interrupt the service but Jesus cast the demon out. A nobleman approached Jesus while He was in Cana and told him about his son who was sick, back home in Capernaum. The nobleman wanted Jesus to come pray for his son, but Jesus simply said to him that his son was healed. When the nobleman returned to Capernaum, he learned that his son had been healed at the exact hour Jesus spoke those words. It was in Capernaum where Jesus was approached by a Centurion who had a servant who was sick. Knowing that Jesus was a busy man, he didn't ask Jesus to come to his home; he simply said to Jesus, "I know a man of authority when I see one, and all you have to do is speak the word." This Roman Centurion's faith so impressed Jesus that He said he had not seen such great faith in all of Israel. The man who was sick of the palsy was healed here when four of his friends made sure he got to Jesus. Mark 1:34 sums up the ministry of Jesus in Capernaum by saying, "And He healed many that were sick of divers diseases and cast out many devils."

While some in Capernaum accepted Jesus, many did not. In a prophetic rebuke, Jesus told them that if Sodom had seen the mighty works they had witnessed, Sodom would not have been destroyed, clearly implying that Sodom would have repented. Unfortunately, Capernaum as a whole did not repent even though Jesus spent considerable time with them. It was not just the sinners who rejected Jesus, but the Pharisees seemed to be His worst critics. How sad that a person can be so religious and yet be so lost.

It is believed that Capernaum was destroyed by a massive earthquake in 749 A.D. and remained hidden for almost a thousand years. The prophecy of Jesus concerning this area was fulfilled, including the destruction of the towns of Bethsaida and Chorazin.

When you visit Capernaum today, you are struck by the impressive ruins of a synagogue and the home where Peter is said to have lived. As you walk the streets, it is an almost overwhelming feeling to contemplate everything that happened here; the miracles and the ordinary everyday conversations that were part of life. If these stones could speak, what a story they could tell.

~ The Mount Of Beatitudes ~

Less than two miles from the city of Capernaum, you find the Mount of Beatitudes, one of the most scenic places on the northwest coast of the Sea of Galilee. A beautiful eight-sided chapel sits near the top of the hill, with each side representing the eight beatitudes.

There are several places around the chapel where groups gather and spend time remembering the powerful sermon Jesus preached here. However, there is one place that I always try to secure for a devotional, because, in my mind, it would have been close to where Jesus preached. If you stand with your back to the chapel, facing the Sea of Galilee, there is an area with several large boulders on the edge of the hill. The mount gently slopes down to the Sea providing an almost natural amphitheater. The rocks would have provided a place for Jesus and His disciples to sit and rest between the times He ministered to the people. It is a beautiful place where I close my eyes and imagine.

An ancient pathway off to one side provides an access route from the Sea of Galilee to the top of the mount that has been there for as long as anyone can remember. Is it possible that Jesus used this path on His way to deliver this sermon?

The beatitudes are simple and to the point, yet unbelievably powerful in their content. In a matter of a few minutes, Jesus provided we ministers with enough material to preach thousands of sermons.

Blessed are the poor in spirit: for theirs is the kingdom of heaven.

Blessed are they that mourn: for they shall be comforted.

Blessed are the meek: for they shall inherit the earth.

Blessed are they which do hunger and thirst after righteousness: for they shall be filled.

Blessed are the merciful: for they shall obtain mercy.

Blessed are the pure in heart: for they shall see God.

Blessed are the peacemakers: for they shall be called the children of God.

Blessed are they which are persecuted for righteousness' sake: for theirs is the kingdom of heaven.

When I was a child, a long time ago, in a land far, far away, the school I attended began each day with prayer, along with time to memorize Bible verses. Awards were given based on the number of verses you learned. I still have a Bible the school gave me based on the verses I memorized. I also have a plaque I earned that contained one of the beatitudes; "Blessed are the pure in heart, for they shall see God." Do you have a favorite beatitude?

As you can imagine, when I visit the Mount of Beatitudes, it is a powerful experience for me. Not only am I standing where Jesus preached, but to have a beautiful memory from my childhood that is connected to this place is at times an emotional moment. It is truly one of those times when the Bible comes to life.

~ The Pool Of Siloam ~

My first visit to the Pool of Siloam was in 1970. On a more recent visit, I went into a shop near the pool to purchase souvenirs. I struck up a conversation with the owner about my first visit, to which he remarked, "I thought I recognized you!"

While preparing this devotional, I was surprised to learn that the word "Siloam" is only found three times in the Bible. Two of those times, it refers to a pool of water, both found in John chapter 9, and the third time it refers to a tower that fell, found in Luke chapter 13.

The water for the pool comes from the Gihon Spring, located in the Kidron Valley, all of which are significant places in Bible history. Solomon was anointed King by the waters of the Gihon Spring. The spring and the pool were the primary sources of water for many years. Jesus crossed the brook in the Kidron Valley on His way to the Garden of Gethsemane. Although the spelling is different, the reference in Nehemiah 3:15 seems to be talking about the same pool next to the King's Garden in the city of David.

Having a source of water became critical during the time of Hezekiah. In preparation for the impending invasion by Sennacherib, Hezekiah had a tunnel cut through solid rock to ensure they would have water during the siege. At 1,750 feet in length, it was a marvel of engineering. Working from both ends to finish the job more quickly, the accuracy of their labor is incredible, even by modern standards. I have made the steep descent from the city of David, past the fallen towers of Siloam, to the place where Solomon was crowned King, and then walked through the water-filled tunnel that comes out at what was thought for many years to be the original pool of Siloam. The tunnel is narrow, the water is cool, it is pitch black except for a small light you carry with you, and it is one of the most memorable things I've done in all my travels.

People travel from all over the world to wash in the Pool of Siloam that I first visited fifty-two years ago, believing there is healing power in the water. The healing power was and still is in Jesus. Another pool, now believed to be the one mentioned in the Bible, was discovered quite by accident in 2004. It is less than two hundred feet from the previous pool.

While most associate the pool with the place where Jesus told the blind man to go and wash his eyes, something of greater significance happened that the casual Bible reader may not notice. The water from the Pool of Siloam was used for a special ceremony during the Feast of Tabernacles, or Feast of Booths. It was a time to celebrate their deliverance from Egyptian bondage. Observed in the fall of the year, it is like a Jewish Thanksgiving. Every morning during that feast, a priest would go to the Pool of Siloam, fill a vessel with water, and bring it back to the altar at the temple. The people would shout and recite Psalms 113-118. That priest would then pour out the water on the west side of the altar, while another priest would pour out a drink offering of wine on the east side.

This ritual was not repeated on the eighth and final day of the feast. John 7:37-39 tells us what happened just a few months before Jesus was crucified. "In the last day, that great day of the feast, Jesus stood and cried, saying, If any man thirst, let him come unto Me, and drink. He that believeth on Me, as the scripture hath said, out of his belly shall flow rivers of living water. But this spake He of the Spirit, which they that believe on Him should receive. for the Holy Ghost was not yet given; because that Jesus was not yet glorified."

On the one day of the feast when no water offering was made, Jesus said the "water" He offered, "the Holy Ghost," is better than the waters of Siloam. Jewish listeners understood that Jesus was identifying Himself with the Rock in the wilderness that gave water to their ancestors many years before. (1 Corinthians 10:4)

His words were greeted with a mixed response. The chief priests and the Pharisees wanted to kill Him, but many others were convinced that He was a prophet, and some even acknowledged that He was the Christ. Have you tasted of these waters?

~ Samaria ~

Most people probably associate Samaria with two notable stories in the Bible. One is a well and a divine detour that Jesus made. In John chapter 4, we are told about a deliberate meeting Jesus had in Sychar with a woman at Jacob's well. Jesus had previously said, "I must needs go through Samaria." The second story is of a kind-hearted Samaritan who took the time to help someone in need when the religious community chose to ignore him.

Samaria is more of a region than just one locality. From its earliest mention in the Old Testament, Samaria is almost always associated with wickedness and sin. Ahab and Jezebel lived there and were responsible for numerous evil acts, including the murder of a man for no other reason than they wanted his vineyard.

Samaria is also the scene of a famine and four lepers. Benhadad, king of Syria had besieged Samaria. All supplies were cut off which eventually led to them having nothing to eat. Two women agreed to eat their own children in a gruesome attempt to ward off death. One kept the bargain; the other did not. During this horrible time, four lepers realized that while there was no food in Samaria, there was plenty of food in the Syrian army camp. To stay where they were meant certain death. 2 Kings 7:3 records the question they posed to each other, "Why sit we here until we die?"

Samaria is mentioned in Amos chapter 6 in conjunction with God's judgment that is being unleased on that area, "woe unto them which are at ease in Zion." Then, in Amos 7:8, a "plumb line" is mentioned. To sum that up briefly, God told them He has a straight and true measure. While the world may often adapt its standard according to what is commonly accepted at that point in time, we will ultimately be judged according to God's holy standard of measurement.

The wickedness and the reputation of Samaria carried over into the New Testament, as you can see from the attitude that even the disciples had towards the inhabitants of that area. The negative reaction to the Samaritans dates back to when many of the Jews were carried into Assyrian captivity. Some who remained behind intermarried with their invaders. This half-Jew, half-Gentile race was frowned upon. That's why the parable Jesus gave concerning the "Good Samaritan" is so important. God has a different "plumbline" that He uses to measure us.

The woman Jesus met at the well also fell into the category of what the world considered the "lesser desirables." She had been married five times and was not married to the man she was currently living with. And yet, Jesus took time to share with her the truth of why He came into the world. She not only believed, she was instrumental in helping an entire city accept Jesus as the long-awaited Messiah.

When you consider Samaria's reputation, it seems even more meaningful when you remember the words Jesus spoke immediately before His ascension. Acts 1:8, "But ye shall receive power, after that the Holy Ghost is come upon you: and ye shall be witnesses unto Me both in Jerusalem, and in all Judaea, and in Samaria, and unto the uttermost part of the earth." It is significant that Samaria was included in His command to go into all the world. We see the fulfillment of that in Acts chapter 8.

Phillip the evangelist, is having a powerful revival. Where was it? In Samaria.

So many lessons can be learned from Samaria the city and Samaria the region. Decisions made in our past have a way of following us into our future. We simply cannot escape the consequences of the choices we make. The world will often not forget nor forgive those wrong choices, but God can and will if we truly repent. We must not allow our past to define our present or our future.

~ The Pool Of Bethesda ~

The Pool of Bethesda was the location of one of the great miracles during the earthly ministry of Jesus. Interestingly, Bethesda is only mentioned one time in the Bible. John 5:2, "Now there is at Jerusalem by the sheep market a pool, which is called in the Hebrew tongue Bethesda, having five porches."

The story of this man's healing has always intrigued and puzzled me. Here was a man who spent thirty-eight years of his life laying in the vicinity of this pool, hoping to be healed. According to the story, an angel would appear periodically, unannounced, and the first person to get into the pool after the waters were troubled would be healed. This man experienced the healing he so desperately needed, not from the waters of the pool, but from Jesus who healed him right where he lay. Bethesda, "house of mercy," or "house of grace."

For years I struggled with this story. Not whether or not the man was healed, but the story that was the backdrop of the healing. In my mind, what happened here did not seem to fit or be consistent with the teachings of the Bible. It almost had the ring of superstition. I even mentioned this on several occasions to Marlene. In my studies, I read where some felt the incident had been altered by a scribe who perhaps also struggled with this story. They speculated whether notes he wrote in an attempt to explain it eventually found their way into the printed text. With the passing of time, I can see that as a possibility. Since a portion of this story cannot be found in the most ancient transcripts, it is often left out of the more current translations.

There is little doubt that the pool we visit is the authentic one mentioned in the Bible because it fits perfectly the Biblical description. Furthermore, archaeologists have definitely confirmed its location. So, it's not whether or not the man was healed, and it's not about whether the place actually existed; it's about the tradition of why this man and others were even here.

Part of my concern seems to have even been silently expressed by Jesus because He didn't address why this man had been there for thirty-eight years. He simply told him to get up and walk. On one of my trips, I finally had an opportunity to sit and discuss my concerns with a Jew. He quickly answered my question. The "stirring of the waters" was not a Jewish belief; it was based on a Greek superstition. While there are often beneficial reasons for "hot springs" or "warm springs," the Greeks and the Romans carried it to another level, one that came to have spiritual overtones with the passing of generations.

While not exactly the same, you still see people today who travel to the salt waters of the Dead Sea because they believe there are healing properties in the mineral-rich waters. I'm not disputing the value of these types of remedies, but the condition of the man in the Bible goes far beyond that. It borders on the side of superstition, and I learned this was exactly the origin of why these people lay there waiting upon what they perceived to be an angel who would trouble the waters.

Jesus ignored the legend and the superstition and healed the man. I fear too many people today have misplaced their faith. That's why they run all over the world to wash in the waters of a pool or bow down and worship a statue. Too much superstition has attached itself to Christianity through the years which takes away from what our focus should always be on. The story of this man's healing must never be about the pool; it must always be about Jesus. He is the healer; He is the One who bore upon Himself "the stripes for our healing."

I'm thankful that God's mercy and grace reach to every area of our lives, both spiritually and physically.

~ Caesarea Philippi ~

Matthew 16:13, "When Jesus came into the coasts of Caesarea Philippi, He asked His disciples, saying, Who do men say that I the Son of Man am?" Verse 16, "And Simon Peter answered and said, Thou art the Christ, the Son of the living God."

In Matthew chapter 15, after Jesus fed the four thousand, He traveled a short distance to Magdala. While He was there on the northwestern coast of the Sea of Galilee, the Pharisees came to Him, asking Him to give them some sign to prove who He was. Was He the Christ; was He the Messiah they longed for?

Immediately after this, Jesus carried His disciples on what would have been a twenty-five-mile hike. Since Magdala was 700 feet below sea level, and Caesarea Philippi was 1,150 feet above sea level, it probably took a couple of days to get there if they walked at a leisurely pace. There appears to have been only one reason why Jesus carried His disciples on this excursion, and it was most likely in response to the question the Pharisees had just asked Him.

I have literally read these verses in Matthew hundreds of times at this point in my life. I thought I understood them, but on one of my trips to the Holy Land several years ago, I discovered there was a lot I didn't know. Two thousand years ago, Caesarea Philippi was a place of pagan worship. The prominent pagan deity in this area was the mythical Greek god Pan, a demonic, half-goat, half-man creature with horns coming out of his head. In his honor, a temple had been erected in Caesarea Philippi, along with statues of dozens of other Greek and

Roman gods. When Jesus asked His disciples who they thought He was, He was surrounded by numerous man-made gods. As Jesus is speaking to His disciples, I can almost see Him as He motioned in their direction and asked, "where do I fit in with these. Who do men say I am?"

The disciples responded by telling Jesus what others had said. "Some think you are the Prophet Jeremiah; some think the Prophet Isaiah, some think you may be a reincarnated John the Baptist." But then, Jesus did as He always does; He made it personal. "But who do you say I am?" Peter answered, "Thou art the Christ, the Son of the living God."

But there is more to this story. There is a large cave behind where the Temple of Pan once stood. The superstitious belief of that day was that this cave was the literal entrance to hell. They referred to it as "the gates of hell." So, in this conversation, not only does Jesus want to know who His disciples think He is, I can also see Him pointing to that cave and saying, "the gates of hell shall not prevail against My kingdom." Jesus was confronting them with false gods and superstitious beliefs.

In some ways, this seems to have been a defining moment in their life. It certainly was not the first time Jesus had been recognized as the Messiah. Mary and Joseph clearly understood who He was before He was born. To some extent, the shepherds and the wise men understood. We would have to say that Simeon and Anna also knew on a deeper level. You could carry that a step further and say that John the Baptist had an even greater revelation because he was the forerunner of Christ. The woman at the well in John chapter 4 received a very clear response as to who Jesus was, and it came from Jesus Himself. While Nathaniel, Peter, Andrew, James, and John certainly had some level of faith that Jesus was the One they had been looking for, it was never expressed as clearly as Peter's response at Caesarea Philippi. And yet, it still didn't seem to fully sink in until after the resurrection.

While this story has many aspects, I would call your attention to just one that I mentioned earlier. After the disciples told Jesus what others said about Him, He made it personal. "Who do you say that I am?" And that, my friends, is the question we all must settle in our hearts. It is not about what anyone else thinks of Him or whether they accept Him as the Christ. One day, I will give an account to God based on my personal decision. That is the issue before us.

~ Bethany ~

Bethany is usually remembered for the events that revolved around the friendship between Jesus, Lazarus, Mary, and Martha. It was obviously a very close friendship. John 11:2 tells us that the Mary who anointed the feet of Jesus and wiped them dry with her hair was Lazarus's sister. We see the love Jesus had for this family when this same Mary came to Him, weeping after her brother's death, and said, "Lord, if You had been here, my brother would not have died." Her broken heart touched Jesus to the point that He also wept.

The only other reference to Jesus weeping comes a few days before His crucifixion as He is descending the Mount of Olives on His way into Jerusalem. This was the occasion when Jesus was riding the borrowed donkey and when people threw palm branches along the path as He triumphantly entered Jerusalem. He was about halfway down the mountain near the Eastern Gate when He paused to look at Jerusalem. His heart was so touched for this city that He wept.

While these are the only two scriptures that specifically say that Jesus wept, Hebrews 5:7 tells us there were other times when Jesus "offered up prayers and supplications with strong crying and tears." One can only imagine how often Jesus wept as He saw all the hurts, sorrows, and tragedies that are part of life.

Martha was the first to meet Jesus when He arrived in Bethany after Lazarus died. Her words to Jesus were exactly the same that her sister would later say. "Lord, if You had been here, my brother would not have died." Although the sisters said the identical words, have you noticed the difference in how Jesus responded to Martha compared to how He responded to Mary?

I think part of the answer to this difference is found in Luke 10:38-42, "Now it came to pass, as they went, that He entered into a certain village: and a certain woman named Martha received Him into her house. And she had a sister called Mary, which also sat at Jesus' feet, and heard His word. But Martha was cumbered about much serving, and came to Him, and said, Lord, dost thou not care that my sister hath left me to serve alone? Bid her therefore that she help me. And Jesus answered and said unto her, Martha, Martha, thou art careful and troubled about many things: But one thing is needful: and Mary hath chosen that good part, which shall not be taken away from her."

Martha had invited Jesus to her home. We tend to mention Lazarus, Mary, and Martha in such a way that we almost have them living in the same house, but on this occasion, they are at Martha's home. As the host, she knew things had to be done to make His visit pleasant, so she busied herself doing those things. Life will always be filled with things that need to be done. They often occupy our time at the expense of missing out on something better. Mary understood that the dirty dishes could be washed later, so she chose to sit at the feet of Jesus and listen to Him teach. When Martha sees this, rather than asking Mary for help, she instead goes to Jesus and complains to Him for letting Mary sit at His feet and listen while she does all the work. In her mind, Jesus should have told Mary, "get up and go help your sister."

That "get it done" attitude seems to have resurfaced when Martha approached Jesus after Lazarus's death. She almost appears to scold Jesus for not being there when they needed Him. Why weren't You here? My brother would still be alive if You had been here. At this point, Mary apparently did not know Jesus had arrived in Bethany. After Martha tells her that Jesus was calling for her, we see Mary running to Jesus, and falling at His feet she said, "Lord if You had been here, my brother would not have died." I have often expressed the different response that Jesus clearly had to these sisters like this. Martha got in the face of Jesus, but Mary knelt at His feet.

There are many lessons to be learned from this story. While good works are an essential part of the Christian life, bowing humbly at His feet to listen to Jesus is far better. We need Martha's in the church, but we also need Mary's. We are truly blessed when we have both.

~ Mount Zion ~

Psalms 48:1-2, "Great is the Lord, and greatly to be praised in the city of our God, in the mountain of his holiness. Beautiful for situation, the joy of the whole earth, is Mount Zion, on the sides of the north, the city of the great King." Tell me the truth now, did you find yourself singing that psalm? When I think of Mount Zion, this psalm is usually one of the first things that comes to mind.

The first mention of Zion in the Bible is found in 2 Samuel 5:7. It was a fortress just outside the city walls of Jerusalem. After David captured this fort, it came to be known as "the city of David." Zion clearly became a special place to David because he refers to it almost forty times in the psalms he would pen. Only the Prophet Isaiah would speak of it more often, with forty-seven references to Zion. Mount Zion is the traditional place of David's Tomb. 1 Kings 2:10 tells us that David was buried in the city of David, but was it referring to Mount Zion, or to a place adjacent to it where David expanded his city in later years. Recent archeological excavations are unearthing what we now know to be where David lived.

As you study the Bible, you find multiple meanings of the word Zion. As previously mentioned, it was a hill on which a fort had been built. It became known as the city of David. There are times when it has a broad reference to all the Jewish people. The scripture in Psalms 48 takes it to another level, a spiritual level. In Isaiah, Joel, Micah, and Hebrews, we see a connection to events of the last days, of the millennial kingdom, and the eternal kingdom.

Isaiah 2:2-4, "And it shall come to pass in the last days, that the mountain of the Lord's house shall be established in the top of the mountains and shall be exalted above the hills; and all nations shall flow unto it. And many people shall go and say, Come ye, and let us go up to the mountain of the Lord, to the house of the God of Jacob; and He will teach us of His ways, and we will walk in His paths: for out of Zion shall go forth the law, and the word of the Lord from Jerusalem. And He shall judge among the nations, and shall rebuke many people: and they shall beat their swords into plowshares, and their spears into pruninghooks: nation shall not lift up sword against nation, neither shall they learn war anymore."

Hebrews chapter 12 begins by showing us a multitude of heavenly witnesses. Verse 14 reminds us that "without holiness, no man shall see the Lord." And then, in verses 22-24, we read, "But ye are come unto Mount Sion, and unto the city of the living God, the heavenly Jerusalem, and to an innumerable company of angels, To the general assembly and church of the firstborn, which are written in heaven, and to God the Judge of all, and to the spirits of just men made perfect, And to Jesus the mediator of the new covenant."

Mount Zion is where the Last Supper occurred between Jesus and His disciples. The sacraments of communion and foot washing began here. While churches regularly observe communion, you seldom find modern-day churches that have a foot washing, even though Jesus plainly told His disciples in John 13:14-15, "If I then, your Lord and Master, have washed your feet; ye also ought to wash one another's feet. For I have given you an example, that ye should do as I have done to you."

Jesus descended from Mount Zion and crossed the Kidron Valley on His way to the Garden of Gethsemane. It was on Mount Zion where the 120 were assembled in Acts chapter 2 when the Holy Ghost came into the room like a rushing mighty wind and settled upon them with cloven tongues of fire. It was from Mount Zion that the New Testament Church was birthed.

Amos 6:1 warns us, "Woe to them that are at ease in Zion." Joel 2:1, "Blow ye the trumpet in Zion, and sound an alarm in my holy mountain: let all the inhabitants of the land tremble: for the day of the Lord cometh, for it is nigh at hand."

As a twelve-year-old boy, Jesus declared, "I must be about the Father's business." If there was ever a day that we needed to be about the Father's business, it is today. Sound the alarm, blow the trumpet, Jesus is coming, and it may be sooner than we think.

~ The Garden Of Gethsemane ~

I will never forget kneeling beside an olive tree in the Garden of Gethsemane as a seventeen-year-old boy. To reflect on the agony that Jesus experienced in this garden, not to mention the betrayal from one of His own Disciples, was an overwhelming experience for a teenage boy. Although I'm much busier coordinating all the details that go into hosting a trip to the Holy Land nowadays, it is still an emotional experience when I pause beside the rock where they believe Jesus prayed and reflect on the magnitude of what happened here 2,000 years ago.

The garden that remains is not very large. It lies near the Eastern Gate, in the Kidron Valley, with a brook that Jesus crossed over on His way to Gethsemane. Today, the garden is separated by the Palm Sunday Road that comes down from the Mount of Olives. There is a public area that contains the Church of All Nations and a private area where groups can meet and have a brief devotion.

Gethsemane is only mentioned two times in the Bible. Matthew and Mark describe the scene and name the place where Jesus prayed until His sweat became as great drops of blood. Luke tells us that it was at the Mount of Olives. While we often focus on the disciples falling asleep, Luke adds their sleep seems to have been because they were overwhelmed with sorrow. (Luke 22:45) Jesus had just informed them that one of them would betray Him and that He would be crucified. It was an overwhelming moment for Jesus and for the disciples as well. Their concept of what they thought Jesus was supposed to do was falling apart. What did everything mean if He was about to die? What was the purpose?

The agony Jesus experienced was expressed by the heaviness and sorrow He felt. He knew the cross was only a few hours away and the torment He would endure. One can only imagine the full fury of hell as it was being unleashed on Him. This was the moment of decision. We see the humanity of Jesus and the dread of what was about to transpire when there came a moment in His praying when He asked the Father if there was another way for Him to fulfill His purpose for coming into the world that did not include the cross. We also see how He quickly Jesus submits Himself to the Father when He says, "not My will, but Thy will be done."

This moment in time was so significant that John took several chapters, going into great detail about what was happening. John 18:2 tells us this was a favorite place for Jesus to pray. Even though Judas left the Last Supper earlier than the rest, he knew where Jesus would be going.

Two miraculous events took place on this night of betrayal. First, when Judas arrived with the soldiers, Jesus asked them who they were looking for. When they told Him they were looking for Jesus of Nazareth, without hesitation, Jesus told them He was the person they were looking for. When He said that, they fell to the ground as if overwhelmed by the power of God. It should have been evident that they had no power over Him unless he yielded to them. After telling them the second time who He was, Peter, in an attempt to defend Jesus, cut the right ear off of Malchus, the servant of the High Priest. Jesus then heals his ear. If you were witnessing these things, don't you think you would have second thoughts about arresting Jesus, yet they followed through with the arrest.

Amid everything that was happening, I can't help but wonder if, at some point, Jesus thought about this. When Adam and Eve were created, they were placed in a garden. There was only one thing they were told they could not do, but in an act of betrayal against the word of God they did it anyway. Approximately 4,000 years later, we are in another garden, looking at another act of betrayal. We could say the first act of betrayal in the Garden of Eden was against God the Father. This act of betrayal in the Garden of Gethsemane is against God the Son.

Though many still refuse to accept Jesus as their personal Savior, the evidence of Who He is and what He has done is inescapable. While the outcome was never in question, the victory was won in Gethsemane. Jesus submitted Himself to the will of the Father. For us to have victory in our life, we too must come to the place where we can say, "not my will, but Thy will be done."

~ Golgotha ~

As I began gathering my thoughts on Golgotha, the words of a song I remember Rusty Goodman singing came to mind.

Born to die,
A cruel cross to bear.
Born to die,
That I his love may share.
He was born to die,
His precious life to give.
Born to die,
That I might live.

According to Revelation 13:8, "Jesus was the Lamb slain from before the foundation of the world." Everything from His birth in Bethlehem to His agony in Gethsemane pointed to Golgotha. His birth would have been meaningless had it not been for His death and resurrection. In 1 Corinthians chapter 15, the Apostle Paul summed up the Gospel by saying it is the death, burial, and resurrection of Jesus Christ.

In the Gospel letters of Matthew, Mark, and John, they specifically refer to Golgotha as "the place of a skull." Luke refers to it as "Calvary." It appears to have been a well-known place of execution. It also seems to have been close enough to a path or thoroughfare that people could witness someone being put to death as they passed by. (Matthew 27:39)

Did Golgotha get its name from the skulls of people who had been beheaded? There is archaeological evidence to support that such a place existed. Or could it be that the rocky hill where crucifixions took place had the appearance of a skull?

Two places in Jerusalem claim to be where Jesus was crucified and buried. One is known as "The Garden Tomb." As you walk through this beautifully maintained area, you come to a place where you see a rocky cliff adjacent to the garden. This small cliff has an amazing appearance of a skull. For this reason, many believe this is where Jesus was crucified and the nearby tomb is where He was buried.

"The Church of the Holy Sepulcher" also claims to be where Jesus was crucified and buried. Many years ago, a building was constructed over this site, obscuring what it would have looked like two-thousand years ago. One interesting feature of this location is found at the base of what would have been a hill. You can clearly see a rock that has a split in it. Those who believe this to be the authentic site point you to Matthew 27:54. There was an earthquake when Jesus died on the cross. This earthquake, among other things, convinced a Roman Centurion that Jesus was indeed the Son of God. Three days later, according to Matthew 28:2, there was another earthquake when an angel came and rolled the stone away that had been placed at the entrance of the tomb and sealed to prevent anyone from stealing the body of Jesus. Is this when the rock was split?

And then, there is this. Some believe the name Golgotha is due to an ancient pre-Christian tradition that the skull of Adam was found there. The first mention of this is by Origen of Alexandria (185-253 A.D.), who lived in Jerusalem for 20 years. Origen was an early Christian scholar and theologian. He writes: "I have received a tradition to the effect that the body of Adam, the first man, was buried upon the spot where Christ was crucified." In 1 Corinthians 15:45-47, Paul draws a contrast between the first man, Adam, and the last Adam, who is Christ. Is it possible that Jesus was crucified where Adam was buried? Of course, there are other traditions of a different burial place for Adam. I mentioned it in one of my previous devotions. Do you remember where that location was?

While we spend our time debating where Jesus was crucified, let us not get distracted to the point that we fail to see He was crucified at Golgotha, wherever that may be. As the song says, "He died so that I might live." Let us also not forget that He came out of that tomb three days later, triumphant over death, hell, and the grave, and He lives forevermore.

~ Hell Valley ~

The earthly ministry of Jesus is coming to a close. Two specific events around His betrayal and crucifixion need to be examined. One is the denial of Peter, and the second is the hanging of Judas.

Let's deal first with the title of this devotion; "Hell Valley." To understand this, we must go back to the Old Testament. The proper historic name is the Valley of Hinnom. From 2 Chronicles chapter 28, we learn that a man named Hinnom had a son who at one point owned this valley. His name is unknown, but what happened in this valley is well known. At some point, it became the garbage dump of Jerusalem. To rid themselves of the garbage thrown into the valley, they would set it on fire. It is said that the fire never went out in the Valley of Hinnom.

It took on a sinister and evil reputation during the days of King Ahaz, who was a wicked king. 2 Chronicles 28:3, "Moreover Ahaz burnt incense in the valley of the son of Hinnom, and burnt his children in the fire, after the abominations of the heathen." Ahaz not only served pagan gods, he threw his own children into the fire as a sacrificial offering.

The Greek translation of "Hinnom" is "Gehenna." These words would eventually be translated as hell or hades. Hell, Hades, and Gehenna, all come from the root word, Hinnom, which came to be known as hell valley, a place where the fire never goes out, a place of evil and wickedness.

I mention hell valley because of the events that happened around the betrayal, arrest, imprisonment, and crucifixion of Jesus. When Jesus and His disciples were in the Upper Room, He explicitly said that one of them would betray Him. One by one, they began to deny it, with Peter being the most vehement. "All these others may be offended and deny You, but not me. I'll never do that," he said. Matthew, Mark, Luke, and John all record this event. Luke says that Peter went so far as to say, "I will go to prison with you, I will die with you, but I will never deny you." But Jesus said, "tonight, you will deny me three times."

We know, of course that Judas was the betrayer. There has been a lot of speculation as to what prompted Judas to do what he did. Was he trying to force Jesus to become the military Messiah that most Jews were longing for, the One who would break the chains of Roman oppression? The Bible is clear that Judas regretted what he did when he saw Jesus would be crucified. So here we are, one Disciple betrayed Jesus and another denied Him. Peter went so far in his denial to curse as if to add emphasis to not knowing who Jesus was.

At this point in the story, I would suggest that what Judas did was no worse than what Peter did. The difference is in how they responded after this point. Judas tried to give the thirty pieces of silver back to the priests, but they refused to keep what they deemed "blood money." They took the money and bought a field in which to bury strangers. It was known as the Potter's Field, or the Field of Blood. Acts 1:19 gives us the Aramaic name, "Aceldama." The Potters Field was located in the Valley of Hinnom. Clay would be excavated from this area to be used in making pottery, and once the clay was removed, it would become a burial site. It was here, in the place purchased with Judas's blood money, that Judas hung himself. The difference is in how the two responded. Judas went out and hung himself, while Peter went out and wept bitterly.

We all have things in our past that we would like to get a "do-over." Clearly, Peter deeply regretted what he did, and so did Judas. But Peter would repent and become what the Bible calls "a pillar in the church." He would ultimately give his life for the Gospel. For many years he was the acknowledged leader of the New Testament Church. His life has impacted multitudes in a positive way for the Kingdom of God.

As for Judas, he hung himself in "hell valley." He is remembered as the ultimate traitor, the one who betrayed the very Son of God. Mistakes from our past cannot be undone, but where we go from here depends on how we respond. Repent, and move forward with God.

~ The Mount Of Olives ~

What are your first thoughts when you hear, "The Mount of Olives?" For most, it would be where Jesus ascended into heaven and where He will return one day. Zechariah 14:4 gives us a glimpse of what will occur at the Second Coming. "And His feet shall stand in that day upon the Mount of Olives, which is before Jerusalem on the east, and the Mount of Olives shall cleave in the midst thereof toward the east and toward the west, and there shall be a very great valley; and half of the mountain shall remove toward the north, and half of it toward the south." A few years ago, a significant fault line was discovered beneath the Mount of Olives. I have often said that it lies there waiting for the Lord's foot to touch it, and then it will split.

There are two occasions in the Bible where the Mount of Olives is referred to as "Olivet." One in the Old Testament, one in the New Testament. The Old Testament story revolves around a sad time in the life of King David. David's son Absalom is rebelling against his father. His intent was to become the King by overthrowing his father. At one point he garnered enough support that David had to flee Jerusalem. A portion of that story is found in 2 Samuel 15:30, "And David went up by the ascent of Mount Olivet, and wept as he went up, and had his head covered, and he went barefoot." This story ended tragically with the death of Absalom who is buried in the Kidron Valley at the foot of the Mount of Olives.

Most New Testament references to the Mount of Olives, including the mention of Olivet in the Book of Acts, revolve around the last days of Jesus' earthly ministry. It was from the Mount of Olives that Jesus made His triumphant entry into Jerusalem a few days before His crucifixion. It was in the Garden of Gethsemane, at the foot of the Mount of Olives, where Jesus agonized to the point that His sweat became as great drops of blood. It was in Gethsemane where Judas betrayed Him.

Matthew, Mark, and Luke all record what has come to be known as the "Olivet Discourse." In Matthew 24:3, the disciples asked Jesus, "Tell us, when will these things be, and what will be the sign of Your coming and of the end of the world?" Again, it had to do with His return.

In Luke 21:37, an interesting tidbit of information is inserted. "And in the day time Jesus was teaching in the temple; and at night He went out, and abode in the mount that is called the Mount of Olives." Near the top of the Mount of Olives, there is a church known as "Pater Noster." It is just a couple of minutes' walk from the "Chapel of the Ascension," which marks the place where Jesus ascended into heaven. The "Pater Noster Church" commemorates the place where Jesus taught His Disciples how to pray. One hundred and forty beautiful ceramic plates are scattered throughout this church, with the Lord's Prayer written in many languages.

There is also a cave. The way Luke 21:37 is worded, you get the impression that Jesus would often sleep on the Mount of Olives. Tradition says this cave was where He slept and where He taught the Disciples how to pray.

Luke chapter 11 contains what we refer to as "The Lord's Prayer." In the previous chapter, Jesus had been in the home of Martha, which is often referred to as being close to the Mount of Olives. This is the occasion when Martha was busy with housework, while Mary is sitting at the feet of Jesus listening to Him teach. Did Jesus leave Martha's home and head to one of His favorite places and there teach His disciples how to pray? It seems so.

The Bible points out that when David was leaving Jerusalem by way of the Mount of Olives, he crossed the Kidron brook. Jesus crossed that same brook when He made His way to the Garden of Gethsemane. The place where David wept because of Absalom's betrayal, and the place where Jesus wept and was betrayed, is the same place to which Jesus will return in triumph. Are we ready for that day? According to the scriptures, Jesus is coming again in the clouds with power and great glory. What a wonderful day that will be.

~ Antioch ~

Acts 11:26, "And the disciples were called Christians first in Antioch."

Cities have a reputation that often identifies them. For example, The Windy City, The Big Apple, Sin City, The Big Easy, and Hot Lanta. Some of these identifying names are nothing to be proud of, especially Sin City. Sadly, we live in a day where sin is glorified and living right is frowned upon. For born-again believers, Antioch is remembered as the place where the followers of Jesus were first called Christians.

For a while after Jesus ascended into heaven, Christianity remained primarily in Jerusalem, although we know from Acts chapter 2 that people from many locations experienced the infilling of the Holy Ghost and carried this experience back to their homeland. The evidence of this would show up later in the missionary travels of the Apostles.

Along with Jerusalem, Antioch could rightly be called the "cradle of Christianity." The first mention of this city is found in Acts 6:5, "And the saying pleased the whole multitude: and they chose Stephen, a man full of faith and of the Holy Ghost, and Philip, and Prochorus, and Nicanor, and Timon, and Parmenas, and Nicolas, a proselyte of Antioch." From this scripture, we see that one of the first deacons came from Antioch.

According to Acts chapter 8, the killing of Stephen became a catalyst for the church to leave Jerusalem and begin its evangelistic outreach to the world. For a time the Apostles remained in Jerusalem, with Jerusalem serving as the headquarters for the church, but many others left carrying the Gospel message. Some of those places are listed in Acts 11:19, "They which were scattered abroad upon the persecution that arose about Stephen traveled as far as Phenice, and Cyprus, and Antioch."

Barnabas seems to have been the first to grasp the potential for the church in Antioch. He moved there from Jerusalem, and through his efforts the church began to grow. After several years, Barnabas traveled to Tarsus to recruit Paul to join him in the work. It was from Antioch that Paul launched each of his missionary journeys that helped the church expand throughout the ancient world.

It was in Antioch where Paul confronted Peter over the issue of him fellowshipping with the Gentiles, until representatives from Jerusalem showed up. Paul felt that Peter was being hypocritical. Although Peter was a great man, he was still a man. His actions may have been simply a reaction from the peer pressure he felt. We often make decisions based on what others will think, rather than on what's right. In Peter's defense, we must remember that he was the first to reach out to the Gentiles, as recorded in Acts chapter 10.

Throughout the eighteen times that Antioch is mentioned in the Bible, we are given an impressive list of the people who were involved in the ministry at Antioch. Stephen, Barnabas, Agabus the Prophet, Simeon that was called Niger, Lucius of Cyrene, Manaen, Nicolas, Judas, surnamed Barsabas, Paul, Silas, and Mark.

There are actually two Antioch's in the Bible. One was a place of great missionary outreach, while the other was a place of persecution. In 2 Timothy chapter 3, Paul briefly mentioned the persecution he endured in Antioch of Pisidia. Acts chapter 13 gives details about what happened. It seems Paul's preaching stirred up some of the women and some of the notable men of the city. Their envy and dislike of Paul and Barnabas resulted in them expelling them from their city. Adhering to the words of Jesus, they "shook the dust off their feet" when they left. Some of these people disliked Paul and Barnabas so much they followed them to the next city and tried to kill Paul. They stoned him and left him for dead. As you can see, Antioch of Pisidia was not a friend to the Gospel.

But the Antioch of Syria, known as the place where the followers of Jesus were first called "Christians," had a significant role in establishing Christianity locally and around the world. Just as cities have reputations, so do we. What will we be remembered for?

~ Damascus ~

Damascus is an ancient city, first mentioned in Genesis chapter 14. Just as it is today, Damascus is always referred to as being part of Syria. In Genesis chapter 15, we see that Damascus was the hometown of Eliezer, the servant of Abraham. While Damascus is mentioned numerous times throughout the Old Testament, it is more often than not a place of conflict between its citizens and the children of Israel.

Damascus is famous in the New Testament for a remarkable conversion. In Acts 22:3-8, we read his testimony. "I am verily a man which am a Jew, born in Tarsus, a city in Cilicia, yet brought up in this city at the feet of Gamaliel, and taught according to the perfect manner of the law of the fathers, and was zealous toward God, as ye all are this day. And I persecuted this way unto the death, binding and delivering into prisons both men and women. As also the high priest doth bear me witness, and all the estate of the elders: from whom also I received letters unto the brethren, and went to Damascus, to bring them which were there bound unto Jerusalem, for to be punished. And it came to pass, that, as I made my journey, and was come nigh unto Damascus about noon, suddenly there shone from heaven a great light round about me. And I fell unto the ground, and heard a voice saying unto me, Saul, Saul, why persecutest thou Me? And I answered, Who art thou, Lord? And He said unto me, I am Jesus of Nazareth, whom thou persecutest."

From this same chapter, we know that Saul of Tarsus was present and consented for Stephen to be stoned. He was a devout Jew and saw this new religion as a threat to his heritage and upbringing. He set out to do everything within his power to stop this movement of "Christians." We know from Acts chapter 9 that his reputation was known far and wide as a persecutor of the Christians.

While on the road to Damascus, he was confronted by Jesus Himself. Jesus told him to continue his journey to Damascus, and when he got there, to wait for someone who would tell him what to do next. That someone was Ananias, who Saul would later describe as a devout man who had a good report of all the Jews. What would we have done if we were confronted with this terrible killer of Christians, this Saul of Tarsus?

When Jesus told Ananias to go to a street called straight to meet with Saul, Ananias expressed his concern. God then revealed to him the plans He had for this new convert. It's interesting to me that as soon as Ananias met him, he referred to him as "Brother Saul." While Ananias accepted his conversion, many in the church embraced his conversion slowly. You can understand their trepidation with this man who had treated them so harshly and who was responsible for many deaths.

The change in Saul was immediate. Acts 9:20-21, "And straightway he preached Christ in the synagogues, that He is the Son of God. But all that heard him were amazed, and said; Is not this he that destroyed them which called on this name in Jerusalem, and came hither for that intent, that he might bring them bound unto the chief priests?" The people who once loved Saul turned against him. He had been their hero; now, they hated him. The Christians had to lower him over a wall in a basket to keep his former friends from killing him.

Once he was safely out of Damascus, he made his way to Jerusalem, but the Christians there also feared him. They wondered if his conversion was genuine or whether it was a clever trick to trap them. It was then that Barnabas stepped up to defend him. It was Barnabas who would later go to Tarsus to bring Saul to Antioch where they would preach the Gospel. It was Barnabas who would later accompany Saul back to Jerusalem. Shortly after this, perhaps due in part to the lingering effects of his former reputation, Saul of Tarsus became known as Paul the Apostle.

It began with a divine encounter on the road to Damascus and was confirmed by the laying on of Ananias's hands in a house on a street called straight. He who had once been the greatest persecutor of the church now became one of the church's greatest evangelists. His zeal for God would forever impact the world.

~ Caesarea ~

Often referred to as Caesarea Maritima or Caesarea by the Sea to distinguish it from Caesarea Philippi, it is remembered for two notable events. As mentioned in a previous devotion, the Gospel was preached almost exclusively to the Jewish people for roughly ten years. That changed in Acts chapter 10 when God spoke to Peter and sent him to Caesarea in answer to the prayer of a Gentile. Acts 10:1-2, "There was a certain man in Caesarea called Cornelius, a centurion of the band called the Italian band. A devout man, and one that feared God with all his house, which gave much alms to the people, and prayed to God always."

God not only spoke to Cornelius in a vision, He also spoke to Peter in a rather unusual way. Peter is in Joppa, in the home of Simon, the tanner. While on the housetop praying, he gets hungry. God uses his hunger to reveal to Peter what He is about to ask him to do. In a vision, Peter sees a vessel descending from heaven that looks like a great sheet filled with all kinds of food. But there was a problem. It was food that was unclean to a Jew. God told him to eat, but Peter said he would not eat anything unclean. God told Peter that he should not call anything unclean that God had cleaned. This scene was repeated three times.

It was then that Peter heard a knock on the door, and low and behold, it was the servants of a Gentile, people who were unclean in the eyes of a Jew. Now, fully understanding what God was telling him, Peter goes to Caesarea to meet with Cornelius. It was during this meeting that Peter said, "I perceive that God is no respecter of person." After preaching a message about who Jesus was and what He came to do, the Holy Ghost descended upon Cornelius and his household, and they spake in other tongues, just like those who were filled on the day of Pentecost. Peter is delighted with their conversion and baptizes them.

Back in Jerusalem, when word began to spread about what Peter had done, some questioned Peter as to why he would associate with these unclean Gentiles. After telling them the whole story, Acts 11:18 says, "When they heard these things, they held their peace, and glorified God, saying, Then hath God also to the Gentiles granted repentance unto life." This would open the door to the Gospel being preached to all the world, which was exactly what God wanted.

The second story begins in Acts chapter 23. Paul preached a sermon that upset forty Jews to the point that they said they would not eat or drink until they had killed him. Paul's nephew heard about their oath and told his uncle. It led to a band of soldiers taking Paul to Caesarea for safe keeping. It was while he was in Caesarea that we have an amazing conversation between Paul and King Agrippa.

Caesarea, which had initially been a place where Paul could be protected, had now turned into a place where Paul was imprisoned. Hearing about Paul, Agrippa wanted to meet him. Paul tells his story, going back to the days of his childhood, and ultimately telling him of his conversion experience on the road to Damascus. His testimony was so compelling that it touched the heart of Agrippa, but sadly not to the point that Agrippa was willing to change. The words he spoke have unfortunately been repeated by countless numbers of people who felt the convicting presence of the Holy Ghost but refused to repent. Agrippa said, "Paul, you almost persuade me to be a Christian." Almost persuaded, but not enough to accept the truth he had heard. It was from this seaport that Paul would travel to Rome as he availed himself of his right to appeal to Caesar.

There are powerful lessons to be learned from these two stories. First, God is not a respecter of persons, which is good news for us all. Who we are, where we came from, and even what we did, does not prevent God from extending His mercy and forgiveness to us.

Secondly, for us to receive the blessings of a relationship with God, we must accept His forgiveness and change. "Old things must pass away so that all things can become new." We become a new creation in Christ. Agrippa could have experienced that, but as far as we know, he never did. He was almost, but not quite, persuaded. How about you?

The Land Of The Bible

~ Athens, Greece ~

Greece was one of the greatest civilizations in the history of the world. In one sense, it never attained the greatness of the Roman Empire, but in another sense, it surpassed Rome. Greece was the home of Socrates, Plato, Aristotle, Homer, Pythagoras, Alexander the Great, and many others who left a lasting impact on the world. Greece was the birthplace of the Olympic Games and democracy.

During the time often referred to as The Golden Age of Athens, a place known as the Acropolis was constructed. The days of mythology produced Zeus, the King of the gods. He is said to have had a favorite daughter, Athena, after whom the city of Athens was named. The worship of many of these gods found a home on the top of the Acropolis.

From the Biblical records, Athens is only mentioned five times. The four references in Acts revolve around one of the Apostle Paul's missionary journeys. The ruins of the Acropolis are magnificent today; one can only imagine the grandeur of the place 2,000 years ago.

While waiting for Silas and Timothy to join him, Paul visits some of the local sites. He takes advantage of the opportunity to discuss Jesus with the devout Jews in the synagogue. He also takes his message to the streets and participates in discussions with various people at the marketplace. Eventually, Paul makes his way to the Acropolis. While looking at all the temples, he notices an altar with the inscription, "to the unknown god." Was this altar built by the Athenians in their zeal to not omit a god they may not have known by name, or is there more to the story? Paul's education is about to open a door for him to minister.

By now, Paul had established something of a reputation among the citizens of Athens. He piqued the interest of certain Epicurean philosophers and Stoics to the extent that they wished to hear what he had to say. On a rocky mound at the base of the Acropolis, known as Mars Hill, Paul begins a sermon. In Acts 17:18, he mentions "some of their poets." The one he is specifically referring to seems to be Epimenides, who Paul would later reference in Titus 1:12, "One of themselves, even a prophet of their own, said, the Cretians are always liars, evil beasts, slow bellies." Paul was quoting a philosopher, poet, and sage named Epimenides, who, ironically, was himself a Cretan. The paradox of the verse in Titus is this. If all Cretans are liars, then Epimenides is also a liar. If Epimenides is a liar, then the statement that "all Cretans are liars" must be a lie, which would mean all Cretans tell the truth, which then means that Epimenides is telling the truth. So, the statement "all Cretans are liars" is both true and false. I'll leave that for you to think on for a minute. This is what is known in philosophic circles as the Epimenides Paradox.

What was it about Epimenides that caused Paul to refer to him on at least two occasions, in particular the encounter in Athens, Greece? So much of ancient Greek history is shrouded in legend and myth that it is often impossible to glean between what is fact and what is tradition. Diogenes Laertius recorded a story in the third century that sheds some light on Paul's visit to Athens.

Epimenides was a contemporary of more famous philosophers like Aristotle and Plato, who refer to him in

The Land Of The Bible

their writings. Around 500 B.C, Athens was hit with a terrible plague. The city elders were at a loss as to how to stop it. They believed the city was under a curse because they were guilty of treachery against the followers of Cylon, who were slain after being promised amnesty. They tried sacrificial offerings, but nothing seemed to work.

Turning to the Oracle of Delphi for wisdom, the priestess said there was another god who remained unappeased for their treachery. Who was this unknown god? The priestess did not know but advised them to send a ship to the island of Crete and fetch a man called Epimenides who would know how to appease the offended god.

Epimenides was amazed when he arrived in Athens from Piraeus at how the approach road was lined with the images of hundreds of gods; collected from the theologies of the peoples surrounding them. Epimenides declared that, indeed, there must still be a god unknown to them who was great enough and good enough to do something about the plague if they invoked his help. The elders questioned how they could call upon a god whose name is unknown? Epimenides responded, "any god good and great enough to do something about the plague is probably also good and great enough to smile on their ignorance if they acknowledged their ignorance and called upon him."

Epimenides advised the elders to seek a sign from the "unknown god." He told them to graze a flock of healthy sheep of different colors, some white, some black, on the grassy slope of Mars Hill. He then prayed something along the lines of, "O thou unknown god! Behold the plague afflicting the city. And if indeed you feel compassion to forgive and help us, behold the flock of sheep. Reveal your willingness to respond, I plead, by causing any sheep that pleases you to lie upon the grass instead of grazing. Choose white if white pleases, black if black delights. And those you choose, we sacrifice to you, acknowledging our pitiful ignorance of your name."

Although it was early morning when the sheep were at their hungriest and therefore unlikely to stop grazing, before long, some sheep settled down to rest, and these were separated from the remainder of the flock for the sacrificial offering. Epimenides ordered stonemasons to construct altars on each animal's resting place. On each altar, they inscribed the words "agnosto theo," meaning, "to an unknown god."

Fast forward now to Paul's visit to Athens. In his discussion with the philosophers, they heard Paul speak of "Theos," God, which was a term familiar to them. It was commonly used as a general term for any deity, not a personal name. But as philosophers, they would have known that Plato and Aristotle, in their writings, used "Theos" as a personal name for one Supreme God, a God far above all other gods. How could Paul persuade Athenians who believed passionately in polytheism to acknowledge that there is only one true God? He does it by reaching back into their past and the incident that involved Epimenides. He said, "As I walked through your city, and looked at the objects of your worship, I found among them an altar with the inscription to an unknown god. What you worship as unknown, I proclaim to you."

The Cretan, Epimenides, gave Paul the opening he needed to present the Gospel to the Athenians. Paul used this opportunity to tell them that this supreme God, who was unknown to them, that they had waited six centuries to learn His identity, was Yahweh, the Judeo-Christian God. Is it possible that God continues to speak down through the centuries about the issues we face today?

The Athenians put their faith in an unknown god who they believed had saved them from a horrible death. Paul told them about a God who was unknown to them, but who truly had the power to save them. All this was made possible through the death, burial, and resurrection of Jesus.

At the conclusion of his message, some of the listeners mocked him, but not all. Acts 17:34, "Howbeit certain men clave unto him, and believed: among the which was Dionysius the Areopagite, and a woman named Damaris, and others with them."

While the beginning of Christianity in Athens seemed to start small, it later gained prominence. Interestingly, the largest of the buildings on the Acropolis, the Parthenon, at one point was converted into a Christian church and remained so for almost a thousand years. The building that had originally been constructed to worship the Greek goddess Athena on a hill with an altar to an unknown god became a place where the Gospel of Jesus Christ was preached.

Paul's encounter in Athens concludes in the first verse of Acts chapter 18. "After these things, Paul departed from Athens and came to Corinth." And that is where we will head in our next devotion.

~ Corinth ~

Acts 18:1-5, "After these things Paul departed from Athens, and came to Corinth; And found a certain Jew named Aquila, born in Pontus, lately come from Italy, with his wife Priscilla; (because that Claudius had commanded all Jews to depart from Rome:) and came unto them. And because he was of the same craft, he abode with them, and wrought: for by their occupation they were tentmakers. And he reasoned in the synagogue every sabbath, and persuaded the Jews and the Greeks."

Corinth was a wealthy port city in part because of its location, but the immorality of the city also added considerably to its wealth. The Temple of Aphrodite, the goddess of love, was so rich that it owned more than 1,000 temple prostitutes. It was a popular destination not only for sailors, but for those looking to satisfy their sexual lust. Corinth was so notorious for its decadence that one of the Greek words for fornication was "korinthiazomai." Today this once wealthy city lies in ruins, but the remains of a temple dedicated to the Greek god Apollo still stand.

When Paul arrived in Corinth, he met a Jew named Aquila, who, along with his wife, Priscilla, soon became good friends with the Apostle. Not only were they Christians, they shared the same trade. It's obvious from these verses that Paul worked as a tentmaker to support his missionary endeavors. Today, he would be seen as a bi-vocational minister. During the eighteen months Paul spent in Corinth, he took advantage of every opportunity to minister the Gospel.

Paul had success in his ministry here, but he also suffered a great deal of persecution. This persecution from the Jews proved to be a defining moment in Paul's ministry. His decision is recorded in Acts 18:5-6, "Paul was pressed in the spirit, and testified to the Jews that Jesus was Christ. And when they opposed themselves, and blasphemed, he shook his raiment, and said unto them, Your blood be upon your own heads; I am clean; from henceforth I will go unto the Gentiles."

His shaking his raiment seems to be the equivalent of shaking the dust off his feet for those who reject the Gospel. While his decision was beneficial for the Gentiles, it seemed to also mark the point when the Jews began to believe less and less in the truth of who Jesus was. Before long, the church would be made up almost entirely of Gentiles.

Since Paul was the one who organized the church in Corinth, you can understand the love and concern he had for them. In his first letter, after a few words of encouragement, he immediately gets to the reason for his writing. The Christians at Corinth are divided and fighting amongst themselves. A man of obvious influence had convinced many in the church that the immoral relationship he was in was acceptable. It seems that some of the new believers were having trouble escaping their previous fornicating lifestyle. Paul commanded them to expel the wicked man from the church. The Corinthian believers were also taking each other to court. Paul told them it would be better to be taken advantage of than to damage their Christian testimony. Paul gave them instructions on marriage, celibacy, food sacrificed to idols, the Lord's Supper, spiritual gifts, and the resurrection. He was dealing with challenging issues. His second letter gives us the impression that they accepted Paul's correction and repented, which was a source of joy to Paul.

The letters to the Corinthian church are very relevant for 21st century Christendom. The church of today is struggling with many of the same issues that plagued Corinth nearly 2,000 years ago. Division is tearing many churches apart. I remember God dealing with my heart in the early 1990's, showing me a dark cloud moving across America, and I clearly heard the words, "a demon of division." Fornication and immorality are unfortunately prominent in the church and accepted by many. The sanctity of marriage, the sacredness of holy communion, the need for order when it comes to spiritual gifts, and a reaffirmed belief in the resurrection are issues that need to be addressed as we draw closer to the end of days and the return of the Lord. If there has ever been a day when we need to stand for the truth, that day is here.

~ Rome ~

Regardless of which historical account you believe, the origins of Rome are rooted in paganism. Although they became a great world power in their own right, the influence of ancient Greece is undeniable. There may never have been a Rome had there not been a Greece. Names like Pompey, Julius Caesar, Caesar Augustus, Nero, Marc Anthony, and many others are recognized by those with little to no interest in history. After all, "all roads lead to Rome."

First-century Rome was filled with all kinds of decadence and depravity. From the murderous games in the arena where people took delight in watching people kill each other, to all types of sexual immorality; Rome was a city that by any definition was anti-Christian.

On October 28, 312 A.D., an event happened that would change the landscape of Rome forever, both politically and spiritually. The emperor Constantine was converted to Christianity. The nation that had fought to annihilate Christianity now embraced it. In 380 A.D., the emperor Flavius Theodosius made Christianity the official religion of Rome. By the end of the fourth century, ninety percent of Romans professed to being Christians. That was quite a turnaround.

We don't know how Christianity found its way to Rome. Some credit Paul with establishing Christianity there, but it's evident in the letter he wrote to the Romans that there were already Christians living in Rome, and Paul had not yet been there. Acts 2:10 says that people from Rome were in Jerusalem on the Day of Pentecost when the Holy Ghost descended and three thousand were converted.

Since Rome was the capital of the known world when the New Testament Church was birthed, it was only logical that the Apostles and the leaders of the early church would want to evangelize such an important city. While the first evangelist may never be known, we know that over the course of time, Peter and Paul would both make their way to Rome, and it was here that they both would ultimately be put to death.

The Bible gives us the Jewish genealogy of Paul, but it also tells us that he was a Roman by birth. There is no record of how his parents became Roman citizens. They seem to have been a family of some financial means because of the religious training Paul received, which means they could have purchased their Roman citizenship, although it would have been expensive. If they were Roman citizens, a more likely possibility is that they were born in Tarsus, which was considered a "free city," just as their son Paul was. This simply meant that all born in this town automatically became Roman citizens. This would prove to be beneficial to Paul throughout his ministry.

The hatred the Romans had for the Christians is unquestioned and well documented. Nero blamed them for setting Rome on fire and used this as justification to inflict horrific persecution upon them. Untold numbers of Christians were slaughtered in the Romans games. Not only were they fed to the lions, having their bodies torn asunder, but there is significant historical evidence that Nero would tie them to poles and set them on fire while they were still alive to provide light for the drunken orgies and parties he would have. The persecution under Nero and later under Domitian are almost too horrible to even think about.

When Peter wrote about some of the events of the last days, he likened the corruption of Rome to Babylon. The prophetic and apocalyptic implications of what he was saying are undeniable. They would take a long time to fully explain, but the city that sits on seven hills does factor into the events of the last days.

Mamertine Prison would be where Peter and Paul were imprisoned before they were martyred. Feeling unworthy to be crucified in the same manner that Jesus was, Peter requested to be crucified upside down, and various writers seem to confirm that his request was granted.

The privileges of Roman citizenship exempted the Apostle Paul from the lingering death of crucifixion which was inflicted on so many of his brethren. He died by decapitation. And yet, the knowledge of his impending death did not take away the eternal hope he had. Writing to his son in the faith, Paul said in 2 Timothy 4:6-8, "For I am now ready to be offered, and the time of my departure is at hand. I have fought a good fight, I have finished my course, I have kept the faith: Henceforth there is laid up for me a crown of righteousness, which the Lord, the righteous judge, shall give me at that day: and not to me only, but unto all them also that love His appearing." Rome took his life, but they could not take his faith nor silence his testimony.

Many of the earliest Christians were buried in the catacombs, among them Peter and Paul. What is believed to be their remains would later be moved. Paul's body is said to be buried in St. Paul's Basilica, while Peter's body is said to be buried in the Vatican, where he is revered as the first Pope.

I would suggest that rather than focusing too much attention on how Peter and Paul died, or where their bodies are buried, we should remember how they lived and how they impacted the world. Rome tried everything within its power to stop them, but failed. That is still true today. While the world is headed for a time when people embrace the Antichrist, the true Christ will prevail when all is said and done. I want to be among the faithful who will ultimately be on the winning side. How about you?

The Land Of The Bible

~ The Isle Of Patmos ~

By the time the Apostle John was banished to the Isle of Patmos, all the other Apostles had been martyred. He was the lone survivor of the men who had walked with Jesus during his earthly ministry. Although still living, John had become legendary, to such an extent that although those who hated him wanted to kill him, they felt the repercussions of his death would be more detrimental than beneficial. They thought they could silence his voice by sentencing him to the prison island of Patmos. They never imagined they were putting him in a place where he could clearly hear God's voice and how this decision's lasting effects would ripple down through history.

John himself sums up the reason for his exile in Revelation 1:9, "I John, who also am your brother, and companion in tribulation, and in the kingdom and patience of Jesus Christ, was in the isle that is called Patmos, for the word of God, and for the testimony of Jesus Christ." And then he adds a statement in verse 10 that I just love, "I was in the Spirit on the Lord's Day, and heard behind me a great voice, as of a trumpet. I have often said that it's good to be in the Spirit any day, but this day would be unlike anything that John had ever experienced.

I was blessed to visit the Isle of Patmos a few years ago. Patmos is a relatively small island located in the Aegean Sea. The Book of Revelation is the only book in the New Testament where the place of its writing is given. According to a tradition preserved by Irenaeus, Eusebius, and Jerome, John was exiled in A.D. 95 during the reign of Emperor Domitian. His exile lasted for about eighteen months. He was released when Emperor Nerva came to the throne. In 1088 A.D., a monastery was built over the cave where it is believed that John received his apocalyptic vision. A triple fissure in a rock inside the cave is said to represent the Holy Trinity.

For Christians, and even those who do not profess faith in Jesus, Patmos is the place where the events of the end of the world are given in graphic description. We are even given a glimpse of the eternal state of the believer and the unbeliever. While it is not an easy book to understand, it is made easier when you tie together prophecies that were given to Daniel, Ezekiel, Isaiah, and other Old Testament prophets. In fact, one's understanding of the Book of Revelation is greatly diminished if you fail to connect what God said to the prophets. I deal extensively with this in a book I wrote in 2019 on the Book of Revelation entitled, *"Echoes From Patmos."*

Patmos is a volcanic island that remains mostly barren, but that is changing. What was once a prison island has become a popular tourist attraction. Wealthy investors have turned it into an off-the-beaten-path place of tranquility. At the time of this writing, there is no airport on Patmos, but cruise ships stop there, which is how our group arrived on this island.

One of the lessons we learn from Patmos, apart from the obvious end-time message, is that God can speak to us regardless of where we are. While a prison island is not a desirable place to be, if we have our spiritual ears tuned into hearing the voice of God, He can speak to us during the most difficult times in our life. It's not just the mountain top experiences when we hear from God; He walks with us and talks with us in the valley experiences as well. The vast majority of the world would probably have never heard of Patmos had it not been for a divine encounter.

When you find yourself walking through a stormy time in your life, remember that God knows where you are and can speak life into your situation. God did this in another cave back in Old Testament days. The prophet Elijah felt like he was all alone and that no one cared. But while hiding in a cave, he heard the "still, small voice" of God speaking to him. It was here that God told him he was not alone and where God commissioned him to complete his calling. God still speaks today if we will only listen.

~ Ephesus ~

The Bible gives us more information about the church in Ephesus than any other church, with the possible exception of Corinth. Paul wrote a letter to the Ephesian Church, it is mentioned numerous times in the Book of Acts, and it was the first of the seven churches that Jesus spoke to John about while he was on the Isle of Patmos.

Located in modern-day Turkey, Ephesus was one of the most famous cities of the ancient world, some say second only to Rome. The Temple of Artemis, later renamed the Temple of Diana when the Romans took control, was one of the Seven Wonders of the Ancient World. Diana and Artemis were both worshipped as the goddesses of fertility. Historians seem divided on just how much temple prostitution took place in Ephesus. On my visit, we were shown ancient signs that pointed people to where the prostitutes were. If Ephesus was like many of the other port cities of that day, what came to be known as "sacred prostitution" was almost certainly part of the lifestyle of that day.

The library in Ephesus is said to have housed between twelve to fifteen thousand scrolls at one time. The ruins of a theater that seated as many as 25,000 people can still be seen today. Numerous dignitaries visited Ephesus, including Alexander the Great and Julius Caesar. Marc Anthony and Cleopatra spent their honeymoon here.

We know from the Bible, and secular history, that the worship of Diana was big business in Ephesus. In Acts chapter 19, the Apostle Paul is having so much success with people converting from the worship of Diana to

Christianity that it hurt the business of the silversmiths who made idols. One silversmith named Demetrius, hated Paul. When you visit the ruins of Ephesus, you can view a place that is said to have been where Demetrius had his shop.

Years later, while in a Roman prison, the Apostle Paul would write a letter to the church in Ephesus. It is a beautiful and oft-quoted letter. Paul begins by praising God for His blessings. He reminds the church that they "are saved by grace, through faith, not of works lest any man should boast." He speaks of the importance of unity when he says, "there is one Lord, one faith, one baptism; one God and Father of all, who is over all and through all and in all." And finally, in chapter 6, he tells them that when they face the full fury of hell, they need to pick up and put on the whole armour of God so they can withstand the attacks of the enemy, "and having done all to stand, stand." Don't give up or give in; just stand.

Ephesus was also the hometown of the Apostle John for several years. Some say that Mary, the mother of Jesus, also lived here. If you remember, when Jesus was on the cross, He entrusted her care to John. Early church history says that John was the pastor of the church in Ephesus and also the spiritual overseer of all the churches in that area, including the seven mentioned in the Book of Revelation.

An oft misquoted verse is a rebuke that Jesus directed to the Ephesian Church. If you have studied the letters that Jesus instructed John to write to the seven churches, you know that most of them begin with words of commendation, acknowledging what they are doing right, followed by words of correction. In the case of Ephesus, after Jesus commended them, He said in Revelation 2:4, "Nevertheless I have somewhat against thee, because thou hast left thy first love." Most people quote that verse by saying they "lost their first love." But that is not what Jesus said. He said they "left their first love." There is a big difference is losing something and leaving something. If I lose something, I am not aware of where I lost it, and I may not even be aware for some time that I lost it. But if I leave something, it is a deliberate act on my part. I know exactly what I have done and when I did it. Jesus told them to repent.

Tradition says that the Apostle John is buried in Ephesus. That seems fitting because of his obvious love for this area. Centuries later, in 431 A.D., a Christian council was held at Ephesus, that unfortunately, was filled with strife and division. They had lost the unity that Paul appealed for, and more importantly, the doctrinal purity he had stressed.

~ Petra ~

In 1985 Petra was designated as a UNESCO World Heritage site. In 2007, it was voted one of the Seven Wonders of the New World. That alone tells you what an amazing place this is, and yet until relatively recently, it was all but lost in the pages of history.

Most people first learned of Petra in the movie, "Indiana Jones And The Last Crusade." The government of Jordan says there was a huge increase in people traveling to Petra after this movie was shown. It resurrected an ancient place that most had forgotten. While the movie did capture a few shots of this incredible place, no effort was made to depict the beauty of this magnificent "rock city." Apart from the brief view of the structure known as "The Treasury," and the great ride through the gorge, Hollywood mostly made up the rest.

The area around the city of Petra has a long and interesting history. It was first inhabited by the Edomites, who were the descendants of Esau. It was later established as a trading post by the Nabateans, a Bedouin tribe indigenous to the region in what is now southwestern Jordan. The Nabateans are the ones credited with carving out the city of Petra.

Some believe this was the area where Moses struck a rock and water gushed forth, as recorded in Exodus chapter 17. The historian Josephus said the Midianites inhabited this region during the time of Moses. It can get confusing when you try to separate the Edomites, the Midianites, the Moabites, the Ishmaelites, and the Ammonites from all the other "ites" of the Bible, because, at various times, they all inhabited the same area and were frequently the enemies of the children of Israel.

This rock city has been known by various names throughout its history. Petra, the name that most know it by today, was mentioned by Josephus as the name the Greeks gave to this area. The name, "Petra," is not found in the Bible, but Bible scholars believe that "Sela," "Seir," "Bozrah," and "Petra" are one and the same. The geography seems to verify that.

While Petra is an incredible place to visit, it is the connection to the events of the last days that intrigues many people today. Prophetic passages like Micah 2:12 and Isaiah 63:1-6 seem to describe the area of Petra in Jordan as the place where the Jews flee when the Antichrist begins his reign of terror. While it is an amazing place, if you've ever been there, you know that Petra could not provide safety from the modern machines of war we have today, so there has to be another reason why the Jews could flee here and be protected.

In the Book of Daniel, a reason is given, but an explanation for the reason is not given. The following areas are spared from the rule of the Antichrist. Daniel 11:41, "He shall enter also into the glorious land, and many countries shall be overthrown: but these shall escape out of his hand, even Edom, and Moab, and the chief of the children of Ammon." This is where Petra is located and where God's people will be protected.

Jesus spoke about this in Matthew 24:15-16, "when you see the abomination of desolation spoken of by the prophet Daniel, standing in the holy place (let the reader understand), then let those who are in Judea flee to the mountains."

Will Petra be that place? I suppose only time will tell, but it is a fascinating subject to discuss. Through the years, I have said that I have many questions to ask when we get to heaven, and this is one of them. Of course, I also say that when we get to heaven, we probably won't care about those questions anymore; we'll just be happy to be in heaven.

~ Megiddo ~

Megiddo is only mentioned twelve times in the Bible, with all twelve instances being in the Old Testament. It is the name of a place that many would say they have never heard of, yet most are very familiar with, only under a different name.

Megiddo was one of the cities that was conquered by Joshua and the children of Israel when they entered the Promised Land. It was a place where numerous battles were fought. During the reign of Solomon, he rebuilt the city, fortified its walls, and constructed a massive stable for his horses.

When you visit the ruins of this ancient city today, you will see a large grain storage pit that is 69 feet deep and 69 feet wide. Since so many battles were fought here, they needed a way to supply water when invading forces would lay siege to the town. An incredible tunnel was cut through solid rock. This water system is 115 feet below the surface, 262 feet long, and connects to a spring in a cave outside the city walls. You can descend 183 steps and walk through this tunnel on your visit.

The last reference to Megiddo is found in Zechariah chapter 12, where it is mentioned as a valley.

This place is only mentioned once in the New Testament, yet the event that will occur here at some point in the future is on the lips of everyone, quite often making the headlines on all the major news networks. Social media is filled with references to this place. It is a place that fills many with fear. More battles have been fought here than anywhere else in the world. At least one more great battle will be fought here, making all the previous battles and wars seem like a childish playground skirmish.

Located in the Jezreel Valley, it is a lush and fertile land. For many years it was strategically located at one of the major crossroads of the ancient world. The international highway that linked Asia, Europe, and Africa passed nearby. If you controlled Megiddo, you controlled much of the trade industry of that day.

Throughout His earthly ministry, Jesus walked by and gazed upon this place that could rightly be called the battleground of history. I wonder what His thoughts were when He passed this area that we know as Armageddon?

From the time sin entered the world in Genesis chapter 3, we have known this day was coming. A great deal of information is contained in the writings of the Old Testament prophets about the last days, and then there is the Book of Revelation. Beginning with chapter 6, you can sense that we are headed for a climax. Two great battles are yet to be fought. One happens before the millennial reign, and the second occurs after. The battle before the thousand-year reign will be fought at Armageddon.

Revelation 16:14 says it like this, "For they are the spirits of devils, working miracles, which go forth unto the kings of the earth and of the whole world, to gather them to the battle of that great day of God Almighty." And then Revelation 16:16 names the place, "And He gathered them together into a place called in the Hebrew tongue Armageddon." The carnage of this battle will be so great that blood will flow for 200 miles. Those who have sided with the Antichrist will see what a horrible choice they made, but then it will be too late.

Every passing day brings us closer to the events of the Great Tribulation. When I teach on the Book of Revelation, I try to stress this one point. Rather than spending all our time trying to figure out when Jesus is coming again, we should focus on being ready whenever He decides to come again. Not to mention the fact that we may die before He returns. So, the critical question is this; "am I ready to stand in the presence of a holy God?" If I'm not, I need to repent and get right with God.

~ Qumran ~

Matthew 24:35, "Heaven and earth shall pass away, but My words shall not pass away."

After looking at the events of the last days in the past few devotions, you may think heaven is the most logical place to look at next. But, there are two other places we need to visit. The first is Qumran.

While many may not be familiar with Qumran, they almost certainly have heard of The Dead Sea Scrolls. Through the years, skeptics have tried to discredit the reliability of the Scriptures, but the more they dig in the sand in the Middle East, the more evidence they find of its truth.

One such event happened in a most unlikely way. A Bedouin shepherd named Mohammed Ahmed el-Hamed found the first scrolls in 1947 when he threw a rock. The sound of breaking pottery caused him to climb up to the cave where he had thrown the rock. Inside that cave, he found seven clay jars containing scrolls that had been wrapped in linen for nearly 2,000 years. Over the next several years, nearly 1,000 scrolls were discovered spread out over several caves. Since all these caves are near the Dead Sea, they almost immediately became known as The Dead Sea Scrolls.

The ancient manuscripts were written in Hebrew, Aramaic, Greek, and Nabatean. Most were on parchment, with a few on papyrus. The hot, dry desert climate had preserved them. Considered one of the most important archaeological discoveries of the twentieth century, and perhaps of all time, they include documents from approximately 300 B.C. to A.D. 70. Among them are over 200 scrolls of Old Testament writings, such as the famous Isaiah scroll, found in excellent condition. These documents have provided an abundance of evidence that has helped confirm that the text of the Old Testament is astoundingly accurate. The Dead Sea Scrolls include manuscripts or fragments of every book in the Hebrew Bible except the book of Esther. The scrolls also contain the earliest known biblical commentary on the book of Habakkuk and many other writings.

The Dead Sea Scrolls give us confidence in the reliability of the Old Testament manuscripts. This is a testament to how God has preserved His Word down through the centuries, protecting it from extinction and guarding it against error, which goes to the heart of my earlier statement. We live in a day when people rewrite the Scriptures to suit their lifestyles. If they don't like what one version says, they will write a new version with seemingly no thoughts about the problems they are creating. Qumran is important because it shows us that God has found ways to preserve His Word through the centuries, regardless of how much the times have changed.

Who hid the scrolls at Qumran? The prevailing view is that the scrolls were written or copied by a devout group of Essenes, a strict Jewish sect. Their study and preservation of Jewish Law went on in shifts around the clock. While most would not like the lifestyle they chose, they did gain the admiration of the Roman statesman, Pliny, the Elder, who wrote: "They are unique and admirable beyond all other peoples in that they have no women, no sexual desire, no money, and only palm trees for company. Owing to the influx of newcomers, they are daily reborn in equal numbers."

The Essenes believed the end of the world was imminent. They never married because they wanted to be ritually pure when the Messiah appeared. They renounced wealth and material comforts and chose to live a communal life of self-denial. They rejected the ways of the two larger Jewish organizations at the time, the Pharisees and the Sadducees. While most of us would not want to live that way, they did the world a tremendous service in faithfully and painstakingly preserving the Word of God for future generations. God's Word is true, and it will still be standing when the world crumbles and passes away.

A place called The Shrine Of The Book was specially constructed to house many of the scrolls. If you ever visit Jerusalem, this is a must see.

~ Israel ~

To some of us, Israel is the name of a special person; for most, it is the name of a nation, a special nation, one that God dearly loves. I mentioned in my previous devotion that after Armageddon, there were two additional places we needed to visit before safely arriving in heaven. The first was Qumran because it speaks to the sanctity and purity of God's Word through the ages. The nation of Israel is the second place we must visit before reaching our ultimate destination. Most of the places we have looked at up to this point in our study have been relatively small areas when compared to an entire nation, but this nation is unlike any in the history of the world. While the world looks at great empires like Egypt, Assyria, Babylon, Greece, and Rome, all those were just two-bit players to a nation on a much larger stage. That may sound crude and perhaps even cruel, but it's true.

It began with a call to a man who lived in a land filled with pagans. If you study the history of Nimrod and the Tower of Babel, you will find that they hated God and even hoped to kill God. Surrounded by such beliefs, how was it that Abraham heard and understood the voice of God? I suppose that's another question we can ask when we all get to heaven. Regardless of how it happened, Abraham's obedience was a momentous event in the history of the world whose effects are still unfolding.

Shortly after Abraham began his journey of faith, God made a covenant with him. It was an unconditional covenant, not based on the faithfulness of Abraham or his descendants but secured by the faithfulness of God. Genesis 17:7-8, "And I will establish My covenant between Me and thee and thy seed after thee in their generations for an everlasting covenant, to be a God unto thee, and to thy seed after thee. And I will give unto thee, and to thy seed after thee, the land wherein thou art a stranger, all the land of Canaan, for an everlasting possession; and I will be their God." The Bible doesn't attempt to hide the many times the children of Israel failed to uphold their part of the covenant. But as I said, the covenant was not based on their faithfulness; the faithfulness of God secured it.

Years after God made this covenant with Abraham, at the end of the children of Israel's Egyptian bondage, as they stood on the brink of re-entering the Promised Land, some of the last words that Moses spoke to the children of Israel are recorded in Deuteronomy 32:8-10, "When the Most High divided to the nations their inheritance, when He separated the sons of Adam, He set the bounds of the people according to the number of the children of Israel. For the Lord's portion is His people; Jacob is the lot of His inheritance. He found him in a desert land, and in the waste howling wilderness; He led him about, He instructed him, He kept him as the apple of His eye." Through all their sins and failures, they have remained the apple of God's eye.

Let's go back to Abraham and look at another promise. In Genesis chapter 22, God asked Abraham to do the hardest thing any father could be asked to do. God asked him to offer his son Isaac, his only son, as a sacrifice, and Abraham set out to do it. We know God stopped him before he did. Then God said in verses 16-18, "Because thou hast done this thing, and hast not withheld thy son, thine only son: That in blessing I will bless thee, and in multiplying I will multiply thy seed as the stars of the heaven, and as the sand which is upon the sea shore;

and thy seed shall possess the gate of his enemies; And in thy seed shall all the nations of the earth be blessed; because thou hast obeyed My voice."

Hundreds of years later, the Apostle Paul explained the ultimate fulfillment of that promise in Galatians 3:16-18, "Now to Abraham and his seed were the promises made. He saith not, And to seeds, as of many; but as of one, And to thy seed, which is Christ. And this I say, that the covenant, that was confirmed before of God in Christ, the law, which was four hundred and thirty years after, cannot disannul, that it should make the promise of none effect. For if the inheritance be of the law, it is no more of promise: but God gave it to Abraham by promise."

When Adam and Eve sinned in the Garden of Eden, God made a promise in Genesis chapter 3. The promised seed first referenced there, reaffirmed to Abraham, and reinforced through the words of the Apostle Paul, let us know that man's hope of salvation was secured by the faithfulness of God and paid for by the sacrificial offering of God's only begotten Son, Jesus Christ. Because of that, I have the promise of a home in heaven when this life is over if I will repent of my sins, accept Jesus as my Savior, and allow God's grace and mercy to conform me more and more into the likeness of His dear Son.

I really believe God wanted Adam and Eve to experience heaven on earth when He first created them, placing them in a beautiful garden and providing for all their needs, until sin ruined it. But one day, when this life is over, God will bring all His children home, and the grandest reunion ever known will take place. It began with a covenant and a promise to a group of people that we know as the nation of Israel.

~ Heaven ~

How do you even begin to describe heaven? The first thought that most people have is that heaven is where Christians go when they die. It is the eternal dwelling place for all who have accepted Jesus as their Savior. Some throw in angels flying around playing a harp and saints reclining on the clouds. The question is, are our thoughts based on Scripture or what we've heard throughout our life?

Over the years, I've had numerous discussions about where Christians go when they die. It is a frequent topic at a funeral. What happened to my loved one? Where are they now? I always remind them of 2 Corinthians 5:8, where the Bible says, "to be absent from the body is to be present with the Lord." So, wherever Jesus is, that is where the believer will be when they die.

In our quest to understand heaven, we often find ourselves at a loss for words, so we resort to 1 Corinthians 2:9, "But as it is written, Eye hath not seen, nor ear heard, neither have entered into the heart of man, the things which God hath prepared for them that love Him."

We can also add 1 Corinthians 13:12 to the discussion where the Bible says, "For now we see through a glass, darkly; but then face to face: now I know in part; but then shall I know even as also I am known." When we all get to heaven, not only will all our questions be answered, we will see Jesus face to face, and we will know everybody.

John 14:1-3 is often quoted when people talk about heaven. Jesus said, "Let not your heart be troubled: ye believe in God, believe also in Me. In My Father's house are many mansions: if it were not so, I would have told you. I go to prepare a place for you. And if I go and prepare a place for you, I will come again, and receive you unto Myself; that where I am, there ye may be also." But where is the Father's house?

It seems to me that many people, myself included, interweave heaven and the New Jerusalem to the point that if we stop and think about what we just said, we realize we have just contradicted our own beliefs, not to mention the Bible. For example, we talk about streets of gold in heaven, but according to Revelation 21:21, the streets of gold are in the New Jerusalem, and the New Jerusalem is not heaven. Revelation 21:2, "And I John saw the holy city, new Jerusalem, coming down from God out of heaven."

Immediately after this verse, John hears a voice from heaven saying, "Behold, the tabernacle of God is with men, and He will dwell with them, and they shall be His people, and God Himself shall be with them, and be their God. And God shall wipe away all tears from their eyes; and there shall be no more death, neither sorrow, nor crying, neither shall there be any more pain: for the former things are passed away. And He that sat upon the throne said, Behold, I make all things new. And He said unto me, Write: for these words are true and faithful."

In these verses, God is in heaven, and He is seated upon His throne. We see a beautiful picture of this in Revelation 4:1-2, "After this I looked, and, behold, a door was opened in heaven: and the first voice which I heard was as it were of a trumpet talking with me; which said, Come up hither, and I will shew thee things which must be hereafter. And immediately I was in the spirit: and, behold, a throne was set in heaven, and One sat on the throne."

There's no denying that the throne of God is in heaven, but will God also have a throne in the New Jerusalem? Revelation 22:1-3 seems to indicate that He will. "And he shewed me a pure river of water of life, clear as crystal, proceeding out of the throne of God and of the Lamb. In the midst of the street of it, and on either side of the river, was there the tree of life, which bare twelve manner of fruits, and yielded her fruit every month: and the leaves of the tree were for the healing of the nations. And there shall be no more curse: but the throne of God and of the Lamb shall be in it; and His servants shall serve Him." From these verses, and other scriptures, we know this is talking about the New Jerusalem, not heaven. Does this mean that our place in heaven is temporary, and our eternal residence is in the New Jerusalem? Or perhaps, we can go back and forth between the two. I think I prefer going back and forth between the two, along with being able to explore this great big universe that God has created.

Hebrews 12:22-23 connects several Biblical passages. "But ye are come unto Mount Zion, and unto the city of the living God, the heavenly Jerusalem, and to an innumerable company of angels, To the general assembly and church of the firstborn, which are written in heaven, and to God the Judge of all, and to the spirits of just men made perfect."

Psalms 48:1-2 says, "Great is the Lord, and greatly to be praised in the city of our God, in the mountain of His holiness. Beautiful for situation, the joy of the whole earth, is Mount Zion, on the sides of the north, the city of the great King." Mount Zion is a picture of heaven.

The expression, "just men made perfect," should be understood as men, women, boys, and girls who have died in the faith and are enjoying their eternal reward. There will no longer be any hint of pride, insecurity, jealousy, discrimination, or competition. Think about a time when you felt deep love and respect for fellow believers. Now imagine that love and respect being completely untarnished by any ounce of sin on their part or yours. Imagine that love being multiplied to a perfect degree and encompassing people "from every nation, tribe, people and language" who are perfectly united in the one aim of loving God and seeking His glory alone. That's heaven!

In 2 Corinthians 12:2, Paul mentions "being caught up into the third heaven." From that statement, we have typically viewed heaven like this. The first heaven is the air above us where the birds fly. In Matthew 5:26, Jesus tells His disciples to "look at the birds of the air." The Greek word translated as air in this verse is also the same word translated as heaven in other places; the first heaven.

The second heaven is mentioned in Psalms 19. David begins by saying, "the heavens declare the glory of God." This verse is referring to the celestial bodies, the sun, the moon, and the stars. These heavens are visible to humans but beyond the reach of birds that fly through the sky.

The third heaven is beyond the sun, the moon, and the stars, higher than the other heavens. In Psalms 11:4,

Psalms 103:19, and Isaiah 66:1, we read that God's throne is in heaven. In Isaiah 6:1, Isaiah has a vision of God sitting on His throne, "high and lifted up." In 1 Kings 8:27-53, Solomon identifies heaven as God's dwelling place. In verse 27 of this passage, Solomon acknowledges that even the highest heaven cannot contain God.

1 John 3:2, "Beloved, now are we the sons of God, and it doth not yet appear what we shall be: but we know that, when He shall appear, we shall be like Him; for we shall see Him as He is."

It seems that heaven is beyond our ability to grasp. But whether our ultimate destiny is the third heaven, or the New Jerusalem on a recreated earth, or both, it will be glorious beyond the ability of words to describe.

~ Epilogue ~

When we began this journey, I felt impressed to pick a few places that have been important in my studies and travels. There are so many other places that I could have devoted time and research to. My prayer from the beginning was that I could pique your interest in learning more about the places of the Bible and the people associated with those places.

Ultimately, I pray that it will create a hunger to know more about God. For Christians, I pray that you will experience Him in a deeper and closer way. For those who have not yet accepted Jesus as your personal Savior, I pray this will help you make that all-important decision.

Romans 10:9-10 says, "That if thou shalt confess with thy mouth the Lord Jesus, and shalt believe in thine heart that God hath raised Him from the dead, thou shalt be saved. For with the heart man believeth unto righteousness; and with the mouth confession is made unto salvation."

Don't delay, do it today. I look forward to seeing you in heaven some sweet day!

Ronald